# ACADEMIC SPELLING POWER

# ACADEMIC SPELLING POWER

JULIE HOWARD

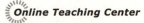 **Online Teaching Center**

Assessment and instructional materials for teachers can be found at the Online Teaching Center

elt.heinle.com/spellingpower

Australia • Canada • Mexico • Singapore • Spain • United Kingdom • United States

Academic Spelling Power
Julie Howard

Publisher: Patricia A. Coryell
Sponsoring Editor: Joann Kozyrev
Senior Development Editor: Kathleen Sands Boehmer
Editorial Assistant: Evangeline Bermas
Associate Project Editor: Kristen Truncellito
Art and Design Manager: Gary Crespo
Senior Photo Editor: Jennifer Meyer Dare
Composition Buyer: Chuck Dutton
Associate Manufacturing Buyer: Susan Brooks
Executive Marketing Manager: Annamarie Rice

Printed in the United States of America
2 3 4 5 6 7 8 9 10   09 08 07

For more information contact Heinle, 25 Thomson
Place, Boston, MA 02210 USA, or visit our Internet
site at elt.heinle.com.

Library of Congress Control Number: 2006921558

Instructor's examination copy
    ISBN-10: 0-618-73180-6
    ISBN-13: 978-0-618-73180-0

For orders, use student text ISBNs
    ISBN-10: 0-618-48121-4
    ISBN-13: 978-0-618-48121-7

23456789-EB-10  09 08 07

# CONTENTS

# INTRODUCTION

In many ways, spelling is the first impression that our writing makes on a reader. Students of English who are not given an opportunity to improve their spelling are at a profound disadvantage when they leave their classrooms and enter mainstream academic classrooms or the workplace. In addition to causing misunderstandings, poor spelling can cause readers, such as professors or employers, to focus on spelling errors rather than ideas and content. Accurate spelling is also a way that writers show respect for readers and for their own ideas and information. To help students position themselves for future success, *Academic Spelling Power* teaches them spelling rules, provides ample exercises for practice, and introduces them to strategies that they can use to continue to improve their spelling after they complete their formal English studies. In addition, instructors are able to monitor each student's progress by administering all of the tests within this text.

## *ACADEMIC SPELLING POWER* CAN BE USED

- in spelling classes and electives;
- as an in-class supplement to a writing or a vocabulary text;
- as an optional supplement for selected students in a class who have a special need for spelling improvement; or
- as a self-study text students can use on their own, as homework, or for personal enrichment.

*Academic Spelling Power* provides students with a lifelong reference to help them improve their spelling. It also provides comprehensive coverage that gives instructors the security of knowing that their students will be guided through effective strategies to help them succeed.

###  Online Teaching Center

Instructors can access chapter notes, supplemental activities, downloadable tests, and the answer key on the *Academic Spelling Power* Online Teaching Center. Instructors must register online at elt.heinle.com/spellingpower to obtain access to the site.

## ACKNOWLEDGMENTS

Many thanks to Development Editor Kathy Sands Boehmer, for her contributions and guidance and to Editorial Assistant Evangeline Bermas for attending to important details. Gratitude is also due for the helpful suggestions of the reviewers of this book: Janet Eveler, El Paso Community College; Mary Gawienowski, William R. Harper College; Sally Gearhart, Santa Rosa Junior College; Susan Kasten, University of North Texas; Besty McCall, Gaston College; and Ann Schlumberger, Pima Community College.

# ACADEMIC SPELLING POWER

# CHAPTER 1

## WHAT IS INCLUDED IN "SPELLING?"

Accurate spelling in the English language means putting the correct letters of words in the correct order. If the last letter is omitted from *quite,* we are left with *quit,* which is a completely different word. Likewise, if the letters of *quite* are rearranged, we have *quiet,* which is also a completely different word. Using the correct letters in the correct order is the most important aspect of spelling.

The study of spelling in this book includes several other areas. One of these is the use of hyphens (-) and apostrophes ('). If you write *ten-year-old boy* without the hyphens, it is a spelling error. Similarly, it is an error if you misplace or omit the apostrophe in *isn't.* Capital letters are another aspect of spelling. *January* and *Saturday* always begin with capital letters. If the names of months and days do not begin with capital letters, those are spelling errors.

## WHY IS IT IMPORTANT TO SPELL CORRECTLY?

When our writing is full of errors, readers may focus on those errors and not on what we are saying. Our mistakes may even result in misunderstandings. Just as we take time to learn grammar and vocabulary, we need to spell correctly so that people will understand and pay attention to the ideas we express. Moreover, a correctly spelled document gives the impression that the writer took care with what he or she wrote, showing respect for the reader and for the text. On the other hand, a poorly spelled document may give the impression that the writer did not care enough about it or about the reader to give the proper effort and attention to the job.

## WHY IS ENGLISH SPELLING DIFFICULT?

The English language has borrowed words from, and been influenced by, many different languages. In addition, the pronunciation of many English words has changed over time, but in many cases, the spelling has not changed. Some people think that a new system of spelling should be established—one that is more regular and predictable. However, that may never happen. For now, we must accept the fact that...

## ENGLISH HAS...

...many words that contain silent letters—letters that are not pronounced. Think of words like *night.* The *gh* is silent, but it is necessary for correct spelling.

...many words, called homonyms, that sound the same but are spelled differently. Think of *pair/pear.* These words are pronounced identically, but they have different meanings and forms.

…only five or six vowel letters but fourteen or more vowel sounds. Therefore, the same vowel letters must be used to spell different sounds. Pronounce the words *love*, *prove*, and *cove*. The letter *o* has a different pronunciation in each word. Another example is the letters *ea*, which are pronounced differently in the words *break*, *head*, and *meal*.

…consonants that have different spellings. For example, in the words *night*, *know*, and *sign*, the sound /n/ is represented three different ways: *n*, *kn*, and *gn*. In the words *kitchen*, *cook*, and *choir*, the /k/ sound is spelled with *k*, *c*, and *ch*.

…rules that have many exceptions. For example, in order to determine if a word should be spelled with *ei* or *ie*, we may remember a rule that speakers of English often learn in elementary school: "*i* before *e* (as in *believe*) except after *c* (as in *receive*) or when it sounds like *a* as in *neighbor* and *weigh*." However, there are so many exceptions—*neither*, *either*, *leisure*, *foreign*, and *protein* are just a few—that we may wonder if learning the rule is really helpful.

In this book, we will find ways to change problems such as those listed above into patterns that we can easily understand and remember.

## DO WE REALLY NEED TO LEARN TO SPELL? CAN'T OUR COMPUTERS DO MOST OF THE WORK?

Computers are wonderful tools, but no one uses computers all of the time. There are times when we must write notes, lists, and other everyday items without the help of computers. We may not be able to use computers when we take tests or fill out applications. In these situations, we must depend on our own knowledge and skills.

There are also times when we must proofread and correct what we or others have written. Even when we use computers, spell-checkers do not always recognize errors. For example, a manager might "run a company" or "ruin a company." You can "draw an angel" or "draw an angle." In cases like these, both words are possible, and only careful proofreading by a human being can ensure that the correct word is used. The exercise that follows presents a few more examples of problems that computer spell-checkers cannot recognize.

**EXERCISE 1**     Read the sentence and circle the letter of the correct choice for the context.

1. I looked at the _____ and decided it was going to rain.

   a. ski              b. sky

2. You can buy _____ at the hardware store.

   a. paint            b. point

3. No one likes _____ neighbors who want to know everything about everyone.

   a. nosy             b. noisy

4. _____ children need special education classes to help them learn.

   a. Artistic         b. Autistic

5. We have an army to _____ our country.

   a. defend           b. depend

# WHAT IMPORTANT TERMS MUST
# I UNDERSTAND TO USE THIS BOOK?

First, you should know the terms *vowel* and ***consonant.*** In the twenty-six letter English alphabet, there are five vowel letters: *a, e, i, o,* and *u.* The other twenty-one letters (*b, c, d, f,* etc.) are consonants. Note that sometimes the consonant *y* functions as a vowel, as in *by,* but in words like *yellow, y* functions as a consonant.

---

**EXERCISE 2**

Circle the letters that represent vowel sounds.

1. m a n y
2. h o w e v e r
3. c o m m i t t e e

4. t a u g h t
5. y e s t e r d a y
6. v o l u m e

*syllables?*

---

**EXERCISE 3**

Circle the letters that represent consonant sounds.

1. s u p p o r t
2. Y a n k e e
3. a l t h o u g h

4. p r o b a b l y
5. i n t e r e s t i n g
6. d e f i n i t e

*syllables?*

---

Another important term is ***syllable.*** *The American Heritage® English as a Second Language Dictionary* defines *syllable* as "a single uninterrupted sound forming part of a word or in some cases an entire word. The word *house* has one syllable; *houses* has two." You need to pronounce a word to determine how many syllables it has. If you do not know the pronunciation, a dictionary will give you that information.

---

**EXERCISE 4**

Pronounce each word and write the number of syllables it has on the blank line.

1. lucky _2_
2. unhappy _2_
3. complete _3_
4. forgotten _2_
5. learned _____
6. agreement _3_

7. force _2_
8. bookstore _2_
9. divisible _____
10. thought _____
11. syllable _3_
12. boxes _____

---

You should also know the terms for the different parts of words: ***prefix, root,*** and ***suffix.*** A word may be only a root, or it may have a root with a prefix (before the root) and even a suffix (after the root). For example, in the word *incorrectly, in-* is a prefix meaning "not," *correct* is the root, and –*ly* is a suffix used to form an adverb. In the following exercises, practice recognizing these parts of words.

together
define
{ prefix
{ root
{ suffix

**EXERCISE 5**

Identify the prefixes and roots of the words in the left-hand column and write them under the appropriate headings.

|  | Prefix | Root |
|---|---|---|
| 1. imperfect |  |  |
| 2. irregular |  |  |
| 3. rewrite |  |  |
| 4. prepay |  |  |
| 5. multipurpose |  |  |

**EXERCISE 6**

Identify the roots and suffixes of the words and write them under the appropriate headings.

|  | Root | Suffix |
|---|---|---|
| 1. quickly |  |  |
| 2. teacher |  |  |
| 3. walked |  |  |
| 4. dangerous |  |  |
| 5. communication |  |  |

**EXERCISE 7**

Identify the prefixes, roots, and suffixes of the words. Write them under the appropriate headings.

|  | Prefix | Root | Suffix |
|---|---|---|---|
| 1. disappearance |  |  |  |
| 2. postoperative |  |  |  |
| 3. misunderstanding |  |  |  |
| 4. bilingualism |  |  |  |
| 5. uncomfortable |  |  |  |

# WILL I NEED TO USE A DICTIONARY?

[alphabetical]

In order to check and improve your spelling, you will need to consult a dictionary often. You will need to be comfortable with alphabetical order (*a*, *b*, *c*, etc.) so that you can find words quickly and easily.

**EXERCISE 8**

Write the numbers 1 through 15 in the spaces before the words to show the correct alphabetical order.

| | | |
|---|---|---|
| _____ garage | _____ material | _____ matriarchy |
| _____ university | _____ barometer | _____ vortex |
| _____ calendar | _____ fragile | _____ planet |
| _____ general | _____ narcotic | _____ satire |
| _____ trillion | _____ quarantine | _____ imitate |

**EXERCISE 9**

Write the numbers 1 through 15 in the spaces before the words to show the correct alphabetical order.

| | | |
|---|---|---|
| _____ economy | _____ economic | _____ ecology |
| _____ echo | _____ economize | _____ eclipse |
| _____ ecological | _____ economical | _____ economically |
| _____ ecologist | _____ economist | _____ ecosystem |
| _____ economics | _____ eccentric | _____ eclectic |

**EXERCISE 10**

As in Exercises 8 and 9, write the numbers 1 through 15 before the words to show the correct alphabetical order.

| | | |
|---|---|---|
| _____ revolution | _____ review | _____ rewarding |
| _____ reverse | _____ revision | _____ revolutionary |
| _____ rewrite | _____ reversible | _____ revive |
| _____ reward | _____ revenge | _____ revenue |
| _____ reviewer | _____ revival | _____ revisit |

You will see that your dictionary contains a lot of information that can help you with spelling. For example, dictionaries often give different forms of a word under the same entry or in other entries nearby.

In the following exercises, look at the entries from *The American Heritage English as a Second Language Dictionary,* and answer the following questions.

**EXERCISE 11**

**cir·cu·late (sûr'** kyə lāt'**)** *v.* **cir·cu·lat·ed, cir·cu·lat·ing, cir·cu·lates.** — *intr.* **1.** To move or flow in a closed path: *Blood circulates through the body.* **2.** To move or flow freely: *The fan helps the air circulate.* **3.** To spread widely among persons or places: *Rumors tend to circulate quickly.* — *tr.* **1.** To cause (sthg.) to move or flow: *The heart circulates blood throughout the body.* **2.** To spread or distribute (sthg.): *That opinion has been circulated widely in public discussion.*

**cir·cu·la·tion (sûr'** kyə **lā'** shən**)** *n.* **1.** [U] **a.** The act or process of circulating: *Opening the window will help the circulation of air.* **b.** The passage of sthg., such as money or news, from person to person or from place to place: *There aren't many two-dollar bills in circulation in the United States.* **2.** [U] The flow of the blood from the heart through the arteries and veins back to the heart: *a person with poor circulation.* **3.** [C; U] The distribution of printed matter, such as newspapers and magazines: *This popular magazine has a wide circulation.*

**cir·cu·la·to·ry (sûr'** kyə lə tôr' ē**)** *adj.* **1.** Of or involving circulation. **2.** Relating to the circulatory system: *The veins are sometimes damaged by circulatory disease.**

1. What is the past tense of *circulate?* _____

2. How do you spell the – *ing* form? _____

3. What is the noun form of this word? _____

4. What is the adjective form of this word? _____

**EXERCISE 12**

**hip·pie (hĭp'** ē**)** *n., pl.* **hip·pies.** *Slang.* A person who opposes conventional standards and customs, such as those of behavior and dress.

**hip·po (hĭp'** ō**)** *n., pl.* **hip·pos.** *Informal.* A hippopotamus.

**hip·po·pot·a·mus (hĭp'ə pŏt'ə** məs**)** n., pl. **hip·po·pot·a·mus·es** or **hip·po·pot·a·mi (hĭp'ə pŏt'ə** mī**).** A large, very heavy African river mammal with thick skin, short legs, and a wide mouth.*

1. How do you spell the plural of *hippie?* _____

2. What are the two ways to spell the plural of *hippopotamus?* _____

   and _____

3. What is the short form for *hippopotamus?* _____

4. How do you spell its plural? _____

**EXERCISE 13**

**hard·ball** (härd' bôl') *n.* [U] *Informal.* The use of tough and aggressive means to obtain a goal: *The negotiator played hardball to get the opposition to give in.*

**hard-boiled** (härd' boild') *adj.* **1.** Boiled in the shell to a solid texture: *a hard-boiled egg for breakfast.* **2.** *Informal.* Lacking emotion; practical; tough: *a hard-boiled newspaper reporter.*

**hard-core** (härd' kôr') *adj.* **1.** Intensely dedicated or loyal: *a hard-core golfer.* **2.** Opposed to improvement or change: *a hard-core criminal.*

**hard·cov·er** (härd' kŭv' ər) *adj. & n.* Hardback: *Do you have this book in hardcover?*
**hard disk** *n.* A computer disk that cannot be removed from the processor.

**hard·en** (här' dn) *v. – tr.* **1.** To make (sthg.) hard or harder: *harden steel.* **2.** To toughen (sbdy.): *harden young athletes by long periods of exercise.* **3.** To make (sbdy.) unfeeling, unsympathetic, or unkind: *Seeing so much poverty and disease hardened the young doctor's heart.* *– intr.* To become hard or harder: *Allow the mixture to cool until it hardens.*

**hard·hat** or **hard-hat** (härd' hăt') *n.* **1.** A lightweight protective helmet worn by workers in construction or industrial settings. **2.** *Informal.* A construction worker.*

1. Of the seven entries, how many are single words (without hyphens)? _____ What are they? _____

2. How many of the entries are always hyphenated (-) words? _____ What are they? _____

3. Which of the entries is sometimes hyphenated and sometimes not? _____

4. Which of the entries consists of two separate words? _____

# HOW CAN I EVER LEARN TO SPELL MOST WORDS CORRECTLY?

Many people, even including highly-educated speakers of English, have problems with spelling. The solution is awareness and practice. You must focus on spelling for it to improve, and gradually, you will see that it becomes easier as you remember rules and patterns you have studied and notice new ones. Then, you must practice by writing and spelling aloud. If you care about your spelling, you will improve it.

*Spelling Word Bank*   Write words from this chapter that you find especially difficult or interesting or that are especially good examples in the Spelling Word Bank at the end of this book.

This pretest will help you identify areas of spelling in which you need to improve and gain confidence. You will study all of these areas of spelling and more in this book. When you finish the book, you will take the test again. At that time, you should be able to check "SURE" for almost all of the items.

*From *The American Heritage English as a Second Language Dictionary.* Copyright © by Houghton Mifflin Company. Reprinted with permission.

# CHAPTER 1 PRETEST

After each item in this test, make a check mark (✓) in the appropriate column according to how you feel about your answer: "SURE" or "NOT SURE."

**A.** Make new words by combining the roots and the suffixes, as indicated.

|  |  | SURE | NOT SURE |
|---|---|---|---|
| 1. study + ing | _____ | _____ | _____ |
| 2. happen + ed | _____ | _____ | _____ |
| 3. lonely + ness | _____ | _____ | _____ |
| 4. occur + ing | _____ | _____ | _____ |
| 5. continue + ing | _____ | _____ | _____ |
| 6. swim + er | _____ | _____ | _____ |

**B.** Write new words by adding the suffix *–er* or *–or* to each word.

|  |  | SURE | NOT SURE |
|---|---|---|---|
| 1. process | _____ | _____ | _____ |
| 2. translate | _____ | _____ | _____ |
| 3. perform | _____ | _____ | _____ |
| 4. observe | _____ | _____ | _____ |

**C.** Complete each word by adding the suffix *–yze*, *–ise*, or *–ize*.

|  |  | SURE | NOT SURE |
|---|---|---|---|
| 1. real | _____ | _____ | _____ |
| 2. organ | _____ | _____ | _____ |
| 3. surpr | _____ | _____ | _____ |
| 4. paral | _____ | _____ | _____ |

**D.** Write the American spelling for each of these British words.

|  |  | SURE | NOT SURE |
|---|---|---|---|
| 1. centre | _____ | _____ | _____ |
| 2. behaviour | _____ | _____ | _____ |
| 3. programme | _____ | _____ | _____ |
| 4. defence | _____ | _____ | _____ |

**E.** Circle the letter of the correct phrase.

|  |  | SURE | NOT SURE |
|---|---|---|---|
| 1. a. a forty-years-old man | b. a forty-year-old man | _____ | _____ |
| 2. a. one-and-one-half hours | b. one and one-half hours | _____ | _____ |
| 3. a. a well-known man | b. a well known man | _____ | _____ |
| 4. a. a man who's well-known | b. a man who's well known | _____ | _____ |

**F.** Circle the letter of the word that is correctly spelled.

|  |  | SURE | NOT SURE |
|---|---|---|---|
| 1. a. gorgeous | b. gorgous | _____ | _____ |
| 2. a. mysteryous | b. mysterious | _____ | _____ |
| 3. a. outrageous | b. outragous | _____ | _____ |
| 4. a. ambitous | b. ambitious | _____ | _____ |
| 5. a. conceive | b. concieve | _____ | _____ |
| 6. a. exaggerate | b. exagerate | _____ | _____ |
| 7. a. maintenance | b. maintenence | _____ | _____ |
| 8. a. referance | b. reference | _____ | _____ |
| 9. a. imoral | b. immoral | _____ | _____ |
| 10. a. misspell | b. mispell | _____ | _____ |
| 11. a. unecessary | b. unnecessary | _____ | _____ |
| 12. a. missconduct | b. misconduct | _____ | _____ |

**G.** Write new words by adding –*able* or –*ible*.

|  |  | SURE | NOT SURE |
|---|---|---|---|
| 1. notice | _____ | _____ | _____ |
| 2. vis | _____ | _____ | _____ |
| 3. accept | _____ | _____ | _____ |
| 4. elig | _____ | _____ | _____ |

**H.** Write new words by adding –*ion*.

|  |  | SURE | NOT SURE |
|---|---|---|---|
| 1. divide | _____ | _____ | _____ |
| 2. satisfy | _____ | _____ | _____ |
| 3. submit | _____ | _____ | _____ |
| 4. expand | _____ | _____ | _____ |

**I.** Write the plurals of these singular nouns.

|  |  | SURE | NOT SURE |
|---|---|---|---|
| 1. nucleus | _____ | ____ | ____ |
| 2. medium | _____ | ____ | ____ |
| 3. phenomenon | _____ | ____ | ____ |
| 4. crisis | _____ | ____ | ____ |

**J.** Write the abbreviations for these words.

|  |  | SURE | NOT SURE |
|---|---|---|---|
| 1. Avenue | _____ | ____ | ____ |
| 2. Thursday | _____ | ____ | ____ |
| 3. after noon | _____ | ____ | ____ |
| 4. Apartment | _____ | ____ | ____ |

**K.** Rewrite the words, using hyphens (-) to indicate where the words could be divided at the end of a line.

|  |  | SURE | NOT SURE |
|---|---|---|---|
| 1. explained | _____ | ____ | ____ |
| 2. identify | _____ | ____ | ____ |
| 3. blackboard | _____ | ____ | ____ |
| 4. running | _____ | ____ | ____ |

**L.** Use apostrophes (') to express these phrases in a different way.

|  |  | SURE | NOT SURE |
|---|---|---|---|
| 1. book of the student | _____ | ____ | ____ |
| 2. house of the boys | _____ | ____ | ____ |
| 3. work of the women | _____ | ____ | ____ |
| 4. job of James | _____ | ____ | ____ |

**M.** Combine two roots for each item to make a word with the given meaning. Example: study of the stars = *astrology.*

|  | SURE | NOT SURE |
|---|---|---|
| 1. study of time: _____ | _____ | _____ |
| 2. distant sound: _____ | _____ | _____ |
| 3. heat measurer: _____ | _____ | _____ |
| 4. light writing: _____ | _____ | _____ |

Now, count the items you checked "SURE" and "NOT SURE" and enter the numbers in the spaces below.

(There are sixty-two items.)

|  | SURE | NOT SURE |
|---|---|---|
|  | _____ | _____ |

You will not discuss the correct answers now, but you will when you take this test again after finishing the book. At that time, you will be able to check your answers.

# CHAPTER 2

## A. EVERYDAY SPELLING RULES

Be sure that you understand the rules presented in this section before going on to other chapters. These rules will apply in many words you will encounter in the rest of this book and in your daily life.

### dd  nn  tt

### Doubling Consonants Rules

Before adding a suffix that begins with a vowel, double the final consonant of a one-syllable word that ends in consonant + vowel + consonant.

**get + ing = getting**

Do not double the consonant if there are two vowels immediately before it.

**cool + est = coolest**

For a word of two or more syllables ending in consonant + vowel + consonant, double the final consonant only if the final syllable is stressed.

**begin (stress on "gin") + er = beginner**

Do not double the consonant if the stress is not on the final syllable.

**listen (stress on "lis") + ed = listened**

Note: *w, x,* and *y* are never doubled.

---

**EXERCISE 1**  Write new words by adding the suffixes indicated. Use the "doubling consonants rules" to form the words.

1. plan + ed _____

2. begin + ing _____

3. fix + ed _____

4. happen + ing _____

5. sleep + ing _____

6. hid + en _____

7. admit + ed _____

8. snow + ed _____

9. run + ing _____

10. enter + ed _____

11. enjoy + ed _____

12. rot + en _____

13. occur + ed _____

14. shop + er _____

15. wet + est    _____    18. forget + ing    _____

16. hot + er    _____    19. prefer + ed    _____

17. fit + ing    _____    20. open + ing    _____

# Dropping the *e* Rules

For words that end with *e*, drop the *e* before adding a suffix that begins with a vowel.

**ride** + **ing** = **riding**

For words that end in *ie*, drop the *e* and change *i* to *y* before adding *–ing*.

**tie** + **ing** = **tying**

But keep the *e* if the word ends in *ee* and you're adding *–ing*.

**flee** + **ing** = **fleeing**

Keep the final *e* if the suffix begins with a consonant.

**care** + **ful** = **careful**

But always drop the *e* if the word ends in *ue*.

**argue** + **ment** = **argument**

**EXERCISE 2**    Write new words by adding the suffixes indicated. Follow the "dropping the *e* rules" to form the words.

1. write + ing    _____    11. taste + less    _____

2. absolute + ly    _____    12. elevate + or    _____

3. true + ly    _____    13. large + est    _____

4. pollute + ion    _____    14. agree + ing    _____

5. freeze + er    _____    15. operate + ion    _____

6. false + ly    _____    16. die + ing    _____

7. prove + ed    _____    17. refuse + al    _____

8. base + ment    _____    18. waste + ful    _____

9. continue + ing    _____    19. file + ed    _____

10. fame + ous    _____    20. free + ing    _____

**EXERCISE 3**    Write new words by adding the suffixes indicated. When forming the words, apply the "doubling consonants" and "dropping the *e*" rules.

1. glue + ing  _____   11. hit + ing  _____

2. drop + ed  _____   12. renew + al  _____

3. clean + er  _____   13. bare + ly  _____

4. start + ing  _____   14. believe + ing  _____

5. state + ment  _____   15. cooperate + ion _____

6. swim + ing  _____   16. star + ed  _____

7. operate + or  _____   17. flow + ed  _____

8. permit + ed  _____   18. shower + ing  _____

9. allow + ed  _____   19. plot + ed  _____

10. drive + er  _____   20. issue + ing  _____

**EXERCISE 4**    Apply the "doubling consonants" and "dropping the *e*" rules *in reverse* to write the original roots.

1. shipping  _____   11. definitely  _____

2. moved  _____   12. approval  _____

3. stopped  _____   13. later  _____

4. hopeful  _____   14. fattest  _____

5. arguing  _____   15. having  _____

6. included  _____   16. boring  _____

7. careless  _____   17. listener  _____

8. upper  _____   18. improvement  _____

9. bitten  _____   19. scanning  _____

10. scared  _____   20. scarred  _____

## B. SPELLING ALOUD WITH THE ENGLISH ALPHABET

**abcdefghijklmnopqrstuvwxyz**

### Spelling Aloud

The English language uses the Roman alphabet. Many other languages do, too. However, even if a foreign language uses the Roman alphabet, the names of many of the letters are probably pronounced differently. This can lead to misunderstandings. We often need to spell aloud for other people or to listen and write as others spell aloud. In fact, you will need these skills to use this book in your class. In this section, you will practice spelling aloud and listening to others spell aloud.

**EXERCISE 5**    Follow the directions in each item to practice listening to and pronouncing the names of the letters.

1. Your instructor will point to the letters of the alphabet. Repeat the names of the letters in the alphabet after your instructor. Then, say the names of the letters as your instructor points silently to them.

2. When you feel comfortable and confident, take turns pronouncing the names of the letters, first in order, then randomly, while your instructor listens and points to them in response. Speak slowly and clearly.

3. When you are ready, each of you can take a turn listening to and pointing to the letters that your classmates say.

**EXERCISE 6**    Your instructor will spell aloud each word twice. Listen and write the words.

*Online Teaching Center*

1. _____     11. _____
2. _____     12. _____
3. _____     13. _____
4. _____     14. _____
5. _____     15. _____
6. _____     16. _____
7. _____     17. _____
8. _____     18. _____
9. _____     19. _____
10. _____    20. _____

# A·l·b·e·r·t  E·i·n·s·t·e·i·n

**EXERCISE 7**

Each student in the class will slowly spell his or her first and last names aloud, repeating as necessary. You will listen and write the names below. Then, you will check each other's work to make sure your names are spelled correctly.

_____          _____

_____          _____

_____          _____

_____          _____

_____          _____

_____          _____

_____          _____

## C. COMMON USES OF CAPITAL LETTERS

When you're writing capital letters, make sure that they are easily distinguished from lowercase letters in form and size.

### Aa Bb Cc Dd Ee

### Capitalized Words

**Continents, Regions, Countries, States, Provinces, Cities:** Asia, the Middle East, Italy, Ohio, British Columbia, Rio de Janeiro
**Bodies of Water:** the Mississippi River, the Indian Ocean, Lake Baikal, Niagara Falls
**Mountains and Deserts:** the Alps, Mt. Fuji, the Sahara Desert

Note: Geographical features begin with capital letters only when their proper names are used. In the sentence "The ocean is a popular vacation spot," *ocean* begins with a lowercase letter because a specific name is not attached to it.

**Days of the Week, Months, and Holidays:** Tuesday, October, New Year's Eve
**Languages, Nationalities, and Ethnicities:** Spanish, Mexican, Amish

**EXERCISE 8** | Proofread the paragraph for lowercase letters that should be capitals. When you find an error, cross out the lowercase letter, and write a capital letter above it.

Meriwether Lewis and William Clark were sent by President Thomas Jefferson of the united states to explore the american west. He also hoped that they would find a water route across north america from the atlantic to the pacific. The land they explored had been sold by france to the us in 1803. Lewis and Clark and thirty-one other men began their journey in st. louis, missouri, in may of 1804. From late fall to april, they passed christmas and the long cold season far from their families in a fort they built in present-day north dakota. While they were there, they met a shoshone indian woman, Sacagawea, who continued their journey with them in the spring and helped them greatly. They also met many other indians, members of over fifty different tribes, on their expedition. They traveled on a number of rivers, including the missouri, snake, and columbia, and they discovered a variety of new plants and animals that didn't exist in the east. They were among the first americans of european ancestry to see the rocky mountains. After a difficult crossing of the rockies, another mountain range, the cascades, still lay between them and the ocean. Finally, in november of 1805, they arrived at the pacific ocean. They had faced many dangers and made many exciting discoveries since beginning their expedition on the banks of the mississippi river in the midwest.

**EXERCISE 9**

Respond to the items with words that begin with capital letters. Check your spelling and your answers with your classmates, instructor, or other resources, as needed.

1. When were you born? (Day of the week, if you know it, and date. For example, Friday, June 17, 1985.)

   _____

2. What is your favorite day of the week?

   _____

3. What is your least favorite day of the week?

   _____

4. List your three favorite holidays.

   a)  _____

   b)  _____

   c)  _____

5. Name your least favorite holiday.

   _____

**EXERCISE 10**

Respond to the items with words that begin with capital letters. Refer to Appendixes B and C for state, city, and country names, as needed.

1. Where were you born? (city, state/country)

   _____

2. List six states of the United States which you have visited or would like to visit.

   a) _____        d) _____

   b) _____        e) _____

   c) _____        f) _____

3. List your three favorite cities (city, state/country).

   a)  _____

   b)  _____

   c)  _____

4. List three cities (city, country) of the world you haven't visited but would like to visit.

   a)  _____

   b)  _____

   c)  _____

5. Name a mountain range (group) in each of these continents.

   a) North America: _____

   b) South America: _____

   c) Europe: _____

   d) Asia: _____

6. Name a river in each of these countries.

   a) The United States: _____

   b) Egypt: _____

   c) France: _____

   d) China: _____

   e) Brazil: _____

   f) Your choice: _____

**EXERCISE 11**    Respond to the questions with words that begin with capital letters.

1. What language(s) do you speak?

   _____

2. What language(s) do you wish you spoke?

   _____

3. What languages are spoken by your classmates?

   _____

4. What language is associated with each of the following cities?

   a) Berlin _____    g) Lisbon _____

   b) Seoul _____    h) Damascus _____

   c) Amsterdam _____    i) Oslo _____

   d) Paris _____    j) Bangkok _____

   e) Hanoi _____    k) Istanbul _____

   f) Toronto _____    l) Athens _____

**EXERCISE 12**

Respond to the items with words that begin with capital letters. Refer to Appendix B for the spelling of nationalities, as needed.

1. What nationalities are represented among the students in your class or at your school?

   _____

2. Write the nationalities of the famous people listed below. Refer to Appendix B for nationalities as needed.

*Mozart*

*Cleopatra*

*Gandhi*

a) Wolfgang Amadeus Mozart, composer    _____

b) Mia Hamm, soccer player    _____

c) Pope John Paul II, religious leader    _____

d) Pablo Picasso, painter    _____

e) Mao Zedong, political leader    _____

f) Queen Victoria, ruler    _____

g) Frida Kahlo, painter    _____

h) Nelson Mandela, social reformer    _____

i) Luciano Pavarotti, opera singer    _____

j) Fidel Castro, political leader    _____

k) Vladimir Lenin, revolutionary    _____

l) Cleopatra, ruler    _____

m) Akira Kurosawa, filmmaker    _____

n) Mahatma Gandhi, social reformer    _____

o) Genghis Khan, warrior king    _____

p) Carolus Linnaeus, botanist    _____

q) Mohammed, prophet    _____

r) Your choice:    _____

***Spelling Word Bank***    In the Spelling Word Bank at the end of this book, write words from this chapter that you find especially difficult or interesting or that are especially good examples.

# CHAPTER 2 TEST

## TOTAL = 25 POINTS, 1 POINT EACH ITEM

**A.** Circle the letter of the item that is correctly spelled. These words follow the "doubling consonants" and "dropping the *e*" rules.

| | | | |
|---|---|---|---|
| 1. a. visiting | b. visitting | 6. a. shuting | b. shutting |
| 2. a. opened | b. openned | 7. a. goten | b. gotten |
| 3. a. bigest | b. biggest | 8. a. latly | b. lately |
| 4. a. usless | b. useless | 9. a. stealing | b. stealling |
| 5. a. arrival | b. arriveal | 10. a. continueing | b. continuing |

*Online Teaching Center*

**B.** Your instructor will spell each word aloud twice. Listen and write the words.

1. _____    6. _____

2. _____    7. _____

3. _____    8. _____

4. _____    9. _____

5. _____    10. _____

**C.** Find and correct the words that should begin with capital letters. Cross out the lowercase letters and write capital letters above them. You will need to add a total of twenty capital letters.

1. The official language of pakistan is urdu, but english is also spoken by many people.

2. Three countries of the far east are china, japan, and korea.

3. One of the main attractions of chicago is lake michigan and the many beaches in the city.

4. A number of american holidays, such as memorial day and labor day, are celebrated on mondays.

5. The summer months of june, july, and august are when many families take vacations.

# CHAPTER 3

## A. MORE EVERYDAY SPELLING RULES

VERY IMPORTANT: Like the Everyday Spelling Rules in Chapter 2, these rules will frequently help you in a variety of situations. Make sure you fully understand these rules before going on to the next chapter.

### Changing *y* to *i* Rules

When adding a suffix to a word that ends in consonant + *y*, change the *y* to *i*. Study the following examples.

**beauty** (noun) + **ful** = **beautiful** (adjective)

**happy** (adjective) + **ness** = **happiness** (noun)

**easy** (adjective) + **ly** = **easily** (adverb)

**study** (base verb) + **ed** = **studied** (past-tense verb)

When the word ends in vowel + *y*, keep the *y*.

**play** (verb) + **ful** = **playful** (adjective)

When the suffix begins with *i*, keep the *y*.

**try** (verb) + **ing** = **trying** (present participle)

---

**EXERCISE 1**

Write new words by adding the suffixes as indicated.

1. cry + ed  _____
2. pretty + er  _____
3. rely + ance  _____
4. busy + ly  _____
5. apply + ing  _____
6. hurry + ed  _____
7. enjoy + able  _____
8. identify + ing  _____
9. beauty + ful  _____
10. stay + ed  _____

11. lonely + ness  _____
12. identify + ed  _____
13. vary + able  _____
14. display + ed  _____
15. hungry + est  _____
16. penny + less  _____
17. sleepy + ly  _____
18. healthy + er  _____
19. happy + ly  _____
20. comply + ance  _____

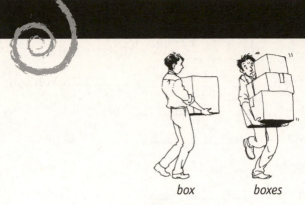

*box*        *boxes*

# Adding −s and −es Rules

To make the plurals of most nouns and to form the third-person singular present tense of most verbs, you can simply add −s, as in the following examples.

**table** (singular noun) + s = **tables** (plural noun)

**read** (base verb) + s = **reads** (third-person singular present: he, she, it)

Add −es to nouns and verbs that end in *ch*, *sh*, *x*, *s*, and *z*.

**church — churches, wish — wishes, box — boxes,
dress — dresses, buzz — buzzes**

Add −es to many nouns and verbs that end in *o*.

**tomato — tomatoes**

Note that other nouns, such as **piano — pianos,** do not follow this rule. Still others, such as **zero — zeros/zeroes,** can be spelled both ways. Check in your dictionary to be sure.

Change *f* to *v* and add −es to many nouns that end in *f*.

**leaf — leaves**

Note that some nouns, such as **chief — chiefs,** do not follow this rule. Check in your dictionary to be sure.

Also, if the word is a verb, we often keep the *f* when we make the third-person singular, as in **golf — golfs.**

Change *y* to *i* and add −es to words that end in consonant + *y*.

**cry — cries, study — studies**

**EXERCISE 2** | Write new words by applying the rules above to add –*s* or –*es* to each word.

1. baby _____

2. loaf _____

3. hero _____

4. tax _____

5. class _____

6. crash _____

7. enjoy _____

8. flower _____

9. go _____

10. tomato _____

11. computer _____

12. match _____

13. volcano _____

14. stay _____

15. taxi _____

16. qualify _____

17. wolf _____

18. dry _____

19. bush _____

20. book _____

**EXERCISE 3** | Write new words by adding the suffixes and following the "changing *y* to *i*" and "adding –*s* and –*es*" rules.

1. fry + s _____

2. fry + ing _____

3. catch + s _____

4. zero + s _____

5. crazy + est _____

6. lucky + ly _____

7. cash + s _____

8. flex + s _____

9. cemetery + s _____

10. bounty + ful _____

11. likely + hood _____

12. sheaf + s _____

13. silly + ness _____

14. place + s _____

15. jazz + s _____

16. merry + men _____

**EXERCISE 4** | Write the original words by applying the "changing *y* to *i*" and "adding –*s* and –*es*" rules *in reverse*.

1. happier _____

2. attaches _____

3. industries _____

4. scarves _____

5. carried _____

6. potatoes _____

7. spying _____

8. avocados _____

9. reliable _____

10. memories _____

11. applies _____

12. toys _____

13. heavily _____

14. passes _____

15. ugliness _____

16. relaxes _____

17. calves _____

18. pushes _____

19. friendliest _____

20. mangoes _____

## B. HOMONYMS

*pair*

*pear*

Homonyms (sometimes called "homophones") are words that have the same pronunciation but different meanings and different spellings. Examples include *pair/pear* and *too/two/to*, There are many homonyms in the English language. The exercises that follow present some of the most common ones.

**EXERCISE 5**

Write homonyms for the given words, using a dictionary to check your spelling, as necessary. Hint: Saying the words aloud will help you find the homonyms.

| | | | |
|---|---|---|---|
| 1. ate | *eight* | 11. blue | *blew* |
| 2. knows | *nose* | 12. meet | *meat* |
| 3. merry | *many* | 13. board | *bored* |
| 4. wait | *weight* | 14. one | *won* |
| 5. threw | *through* | 15. cents | *scents* |
| 6. male | *mail* | 16. flower | *flour* |
| 7. dye | *die* | 17. write | *right* |
| 8. son | *sun* | 18. hear | *here* |
| 9. weigh | *way* | 19. four | *for* |
| 10. they're | *there* | 20. role | *roll* |

**EXERCISE 6**

Circle the appropriate homonym for each choice in parentheses ( ).

1. An (aunt/ant) is an insect. A (be/bee) is also an insect.

2. A (brake/break) is used (two/to/too) stop a machine, such as a car.

3. You may take aspirin to (lesson/lessen) the pain of a toothache.

4. World (piece/peace) is a goal that is difficult to reach.

5. On the way to work, I (passed/past) my favorite bakery, (sew/so) I stopped to (by/buy) a muffin.

6. At high (tide/tied), the water covers the beach almost completely. We must (weight/wait) for a lower water level to use the beach.

7. Is it the duty of rich countries to help (pour/poor) countries (whether/weather) or not they have similar types of governments and values?

8. I (would/wood) like to find a job that makes use of my talents and experience. In (some/sum), I'm looking (four/for) employment in my field.

9. Memorials to those who died are often built on the (sites/sights) of battles or disasters.

10. We're not (aloud/allowed) to use cell phones in class. (Where/Wear) may we use them?

11. In the past, people most often (scent/sent) letters via the U.S. (mail/male). Today, however, they often use computers to communicate with (they're/their) friends.

12. The (sea/see) is an always-popular vacation destination.

## EXERCISE 7

*Online Teaching Center*

For each item, you will write one of the homonyms presented in Exercises 5 and 6. Your instructor will say a homonym, say it in a sentence, and repeat the homonym. Listen and write the homonym, using the correct spelling.

1. _____    6. _____

2. _____    7. _____

3. _____    8. _____

4. _____    9. _____

5. _____    10. _____

11. _____    14. _____

12. _____    15. _____

13. _____    16. _____

# C. APOSTROPHES WITH POSSESSIVES AND CONTRACTIONS

Apostrophes are most often used for two purposes: to form possessives of nouns and to form contractions.

*the neighbor's dog*          *the neighbors' dog*

## Apostrophes in the Possessives of Nouns

In general, the possessive of a singular noun is formed by adding 's (apostrophe + s), as in **my sister's job** and **our city's streets.**

This is true even when the noun ends in *s*, as in **Chris's new jacket** and **our class's favorite restaurant.**

The possessive of a plural noun is formed by adding only ' (apostrophe), as in **the five companies' employees** and **my parents'** names.

Exception: If the plural noun is irregular and does not end in *s*, 's (apostrophe + s) is added, as in **the children's** teachers and **the men's work.**

**EXERCISE 8**    Fill in the blanks by adding *s* or *'s* to nouns that should be possessive. If the noun is not possessive, write *0* (zero) in the space.

1. The government _____ plan to raise taxes was protested by the citizens _____.

2. Our instructor _____ office hours are posted on the door. She is always willing to discuss students _____ problems_____ with them.

3. The Smiths _____ house was sold last month. The buyer _____ offer was twice what the Smiths _____ had paid for it.

4. We were very impressed by the women _____ organizational skills in raising money for their cause.

5. Charles _____ checking account showed a balance of several thousand dollars, so he was easily able to pay his brother _____ telephone _____ bill for him.

6. You should enter all of your friends _____ names in your address book.

**EXERCISE 9**    Rewrite the phrases using possessive nouns with apostrophes. For example, "the office of your brother" can be rewritten as "your brother's office."

1. the house of my uncle _____

2. the insurance plan of my employer _____

3. the car of my friends _____

4. the degree of Dr. Harris _____

5. the complaints of the neighbors _____

6. the economy of Brazil _____

7. the work of the scientists _____

8. the toys of the children _____

9. the report of the company _____

10. the decision of the judge _____

11. the cost of the project _____

12. the designs of the architects _____

13. the illness of the patient _____

14. the answers of my classmates _____

15. the grades of Carlos _____

# Apostrophes in Contractions

Apostrophes are used in contractions (short forms) of verbs to indicate where letters are missing, as in **aren't** (*are not*), **he'll** (*he will*), and **she's** (*she is* or *she has*). Exception: **won't** (*will not*) is irregular.

Note: A contraction is a single word—not two words.

**EXERCISE 10**

Use apostrophes to write contractions of the words. Remember to place the apostrophes where the missing letters would be.

1. we are
2. is not
3. she will
4. they are
5. we have
6. I am
7. he is
8. are not
9. has not
10. do not
11. you would
12. I will
13. you are
14. they have
15. will not
16. was not

17. cannot
18. could not
19. would not
20. I have
21. he would
22. should not
23. have not
24. had not
25. were not
26. she is
27. there is
28. it is
29. they will
30. they had
31. did not
32. does not

**EXERCISE 11**

Rewrite the sentences, using contractions wherever possible.

1. You should not buy a computer until you have compared prices at different stores.

2. She will call when she is ready to meet with us.

3. They did not fix the problem earlier, and now it is a bigger problem.

_____

4. I would like a cup of tea, if it is not too much trouble.

_____

5. He had better finish that report, because his boss cannot wait much longer.

_____

6. We have been trying to reach our friend, but she has not answered her phone.

_____

7. They were not ready for your test, because they had not studied.

_____

8. Do not call 911 unless there is a real emergency.

_____

9. They will not make a decision, because they are not sure of the facts.

_____

10. I am sure you know that I would never lie to you.

_____

Exercises 12, 13, 14, and 15 focus on some common problems in the use of apostrophes. In these exercises, the apostrophe (') does not indicate possession. It indicates that a letter is missing. The possessive adjectives do not have apostrophes. The contractions and possessives in these exercises are homonyms: *it's/its, you're/your, they're/their,* and *who's/whose.*

**EXERCISE 12**

Complete the sentences with *it's* (for *it is* or *it has*) or *its* (possessive adjective).

1. The store opened _____ doors for business in January of 1957.

2. _____ been a long time since a war was fought on U.S. soil.

3. _____ amazing but true that a raccoon washes _____ fruit before eating it.

4. San Francisco is known for _____ hilly streets and foggy weather. _____ also famous for beautiful views and _____ sizable Asian-American population.

5. _____ intelligence and grace make the dolphin an impressive animal.

**EXERCISE 13**  Complete the sentences with *you're* (for *you are*) or *your* (possessive adjective.)

1. When _____ applying for a job, you should present a resume that will list _____ qualifications and experience.

2. If _____ tired during the day, it may be because _____ not getting enough sleep at night. Adequate sleep is very important to _____ health.

3. The genes you inherit from _____ mother and father determine _____ hair and eye color.

4. I can see that _____ busy, so I'll come back later.

5. You should wait until _____ invited before you enter another person's home.

**EXERCISE 14**  Complete the sentences with *they're* (for *they are*) or *their* (possessive adjective).

1. _____ tired, because they helped _____ friends move today.

2. Most people love _____ families even when _____ annoyed with them.

3. The employees plan to ask for a raise in _____ pay, because _____ working longer hours now.

4. Some people let _____ telephone answering machines take messages even when _____ at home.

5. Famous people sometimes have to sacrifice _____ privacy in order to be famous.

**EXERCISE 15**  Complete the sentences with *who's* (for *who is* or *who has*) and *whose* (possessive adjective or question word).

1. _____ at the door?

2. There's a strange car in front of our building. I wonder _____ car it is.

3. _____ physics book is this? _____ been studying in here?

4. The man _____ house burned down is now living with relatives.

5. I'm not sure _____ to blame for the problem. I'm not sure _____ fault it is.

***Spelling Word Bank***    In the Spelling Word Bank at the end of this book, write words from this chapter that you find especially difficult or interesting or that are especially good examples.

# CHAPTER 3 TEST

## TOTAL = 25 POINTS, 1 POINT EACH ITEM

**A.** Circle the letter of the correctly spelled word.

1. a. knifes      b. knives

2. a. studying      b. studing

3. a. plays      b. plaies

4. a. vetos      b. vetoes

5. a. buryed      b. buried

6. a. marries      b. marrys

7. a. foxs      b. foxes

8. a. lazyly      b. lazily

**B.** Circle the letter of the appropriate homonym.

1. Do you know _____ the class is at 8:00 or 9:00?

   a. weather      b. whether

2. The term papers must be finished _____ Friday.

   a. by      b. buy

3. The students took _____ exams last week.

   a. they're      b. their

4. Half of the employees in our office are _____.

   a. male      b. mail

5. Your _____ is listed on your driver's license.

   a. weight      b. wait

6. _____ you like a cup of coffee?

   a. Would      b. Wood

7. It makes _____ to save money.

   a. cents      b. sense

8. The workers have two coffee _____.

   a. breaks      b. brakes

9. Your first choice is often the _____ answer.

    a. write            b. right

10. It's important _____ have a satisfying job.

    a. to              b. too

11. I ordered a _____ of cake for dessert.

    a. piece           b. peace

12. We traveled _____ Mexico to Guatemala.

    a. through        b. threw

**C.** Circle the letter of the choice that demonstrates correct use of the apostrophe.

1. The cat closed _____ eyes and went to sleep.

    a. its              b. it's

2. The _____ boss made them work extra hours.

    a. mens'          b. men's

3. _____ degree in computer science makes him an attractive job applicant.

    a. James's       b. James'

4. You shouldn't talk on the phone when _____ driving.

    a. you're       b. your

5. The _____ grades were good enough to allow her to get a scholarship.

    a. students'      b. student's

# CHAPTER 4

## A. COMMON SUFFIXES FOR NOUNS AND VERBS

The noun suffixes *–er* and *–or* mean "someone/something that does something." Deciding which suffix to use is not too difficult if you know the rules.

*runner*                    *conductor*

### Adding *–er* and *–or* Rules for Nouns

Most nouns of this type have the suffix *–er*.

**teach + er = teacher**

Add *–or* to most roots that end in *t, ate,* or *ess*.

**collect + or = collector, locate + or = locator, profess + or = professor**

However, there are many exceptions, such as *paint—painter, hunt—hunter, sail—sailor, dress—dresser,* and *supervise—supervisor*. If you must guess, use *–er*, which is more common.

Note: When the word is a comparative, the suffix is always *–er*, as in *neat—neater, less—lesser,* and *late—later*. In this chapter, we will not practice comparatives.

**EXERCISE 1**

Add −*er* and −*or* to the words. Write the new words in the spaces provided. All of these examples follow the rules. Remember to drop the *e*, double consonants, or change *y* to *i* where necessary.

1. perform _____
2. operate _____
3. read _____
4. refrigerate _____
5. process _____
6. farm _____
7. help _____
8. act _____
9. radiate _____
10. listen _____

11. custom _____
12. own _____
13. jog _____
14. drive _____
15. invent _____
16. inspect _____
17. direct _____
18. use _____
19. carry _____
20. begin _____

**EXERCISE 2**

As in Exercise 1, add −*er* and −*or* to create new words. All of these examples follow the rules. Change *y* to *i*, double consonants, and drop the *e* as necessary.

1. legislate _____
2. bake _____
3. generate _____
4. buy _____
5. boil _____
6. elevate _____
7. rob _____
8. contract _____
9. play _____
10. lead _____

11. investigate _____
12. sculpt _____
13. write _____
14. sell _____
15. edit _____
16. instruct _____
17. wash _____
18. speak _____
19. dance _____
20. audit _____

**EXERCISE 3**

Answer the questions using −*er* and −*or* words from this section.

1. Which of the words represent machines?

_____

_____

2. Which represent occupations in the performing and visual arts?

_____

_____

3. Which represent jobs in publishing?

_____

_____

4. Which represent roles you have played, jobs you have had, or activities you have done?

_____

_____

Many nouns in English can be formed by adding −*ion* to verbs. There are several ways to spell this suffix, but it is always pronounced the same. Here are a few guidelines to assist you in spelling these words.

*addition, subtraction, multiplication, division*

## Adding *−ion* Rules

Add −*ion* to verbs that end in *s* and *t*.

>   **express + ion = expression, subtract + ion = subtraction**

If the verbs end in *se* or *te,* drop the *e* before adding −*ion*.

>   **confuse + ion = confusion, pollute + ion = pollution**

If the verb ends in *d* or *de,* drop the *d* or *de* and add −*sion*.

>   **divide + ion = division**

If adding the suffix results in also adding an extra vowel or syllable, add −*tion*. You'll need to pronounce the word in order to determine this.

>   **add + ion = addition** (extra *i* is added for ease in pronunciation)

>   **multiply + ion = multiplication** (extra *ca* is added; also *y* is changed to *i*)

If adding the suffix results in the pronunciation of "mission," the spelling will be −*ssion*. Pronounce the word to determine this.

>   **admit + ion = admission**

There are many words to which no rules can be applied. Because −*tion* is the most frequent, use this spelling when you're not sure.

**EXERCISE 4**    Make new words from the verbs by adding a form of −*ion*. All of these examples follow the rules above.

1. act  _____
2. perfect  _____
3. impress  _____
4. discuss  _____
5. conclude  _____
6. contract  _____
7. satisfy  _____
8. edit  _____
9. supervise  _____
10. include  _____

11. televise  _____
12. explode  _____
13. decide  _____
14. permit  _____
15. adopt  _____
16. immigrate  _____
17. instruct  _____
18. imitate  _____
19. persuade  _____
20. operate  _____

**EXERCISE 5**    As in Exercise 4, make new words by adding forms of −*ion*. These examples follow the rules.

1. revise  _____
2. register  _____
3. examine  _____
4. invade  _____
5. expand  _____
6. confess  _____
7. confuse  _____
8. evaluate  _____
9. submit  _____
10. erode  _____

11. dedicate  _____
12. possess  _____
13. direct  _____
14. educate  _____
15. devote  _____
16. transmit  _____
17. interpret  _____
18. cooperate  _____
19. obsess  _____
20. comprehend  _____

Adding the suffix −*ize* to a root is a common way to form a verb. There are two variations: −*ise* and −*yze*. The suffix −*ize* is by far the most frequent, so if you memorize the shorter lists of words that end in −*ise* and −*yze*, you will be able to spell verbs of this type correctly all or most of the time.

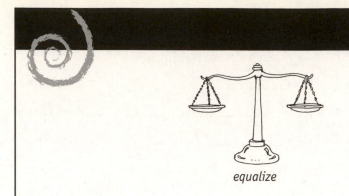

*equalize*

# Adding −*ize*, −*ise*, or −*yze* Rules for Verbs

Most verbs of this type end in −*ize*, such as **socialize**.

Fewer verbs end in −*ise*, so try to memorize these common examples:

| | |
|---|---|
| **advertise** | **exercise** |
| **compromise** | **revise** |
| **despise** | **supervise** |
| **disguise** | **surprise** |

Very few verbs end in −*yze*. Remember these common examples:

**analyze**

**paralyze**

*Note that some of these verbs can also be used as nouns. Common examples include* surprise, compromise, *and* disguise.

**EXERCISE 6**

Study the lists in the chart above. Then, rewrite each root with the correct suffix, −*ize*, −*ise*, or −*yze*. Try not to look at the chart until you are finished with the exercise.

1. national _____    10. surpr _____

2. econom _____    11. exerc _____

3. superv _____    12. organ _____

4. final _____    13. maxim _____

5. anal _____    14. alphabet _____

6. terror _____    15. desp _____

7. civil _____    16. modern _____

8. comprom _____    17. recogn _____

9. advert _____    18. categor _____

**EXERCISE 7** | As in Exercise 6, create new words by adding *−ise*, *−ize*, or *−yze* to the roots.

1. personal _____

2. mobil _____

3. harmon _____

4. capital _____

5. disgu _____

6. special _____

7. apolog _____

8. paral _____

9. fertil _____

10. equal _____

11. hospital _____

12. rev _____

13. critic _____

14. dramat _____

15. public _____

16. minim _____

## B. SILENT LETTERS

English has many silent letters—letters that are not pronounced but are part of correct spelling. The most common example of a silent vowel is the *e* in words like *make, life,* and *store.* Common examples of silent consonants include the *t* in *often* and the *gh* in *night.*

### A Few Silent Letter Rules

*k* and *g* are usually silent when followed by *n,* as in **knock** and **gnat.**

*b* is usually silent after *m,* as in **lamb,** and before *t,* as in **doubt.**

(Common exceptions include *September, November,* and *obtain.*)

*h* is silent after *g,* as in **ghost,** and after *r,* as in **rhyme.**

*gh* is silent before *t,* as in **night,** in the middle of a word, as in **neighbor,** and at the end of a word, as in **sigh.**

*d* is silent before *g,* as in **judge.**

final *e* is usually silent when it is preceded by vowel + consonant(s), as in **table** and **wife.**

Remember that many silent letters do not follow any rules. You will learn about most silent letters through your practice in writing and speaking English.

*knot*

**EXERCISE 8**   Identify the silent letters in the following words and write them in the spaces provided. These examples follow the rules above.

1. comb _____        4. knife _____        7. ghoul _____

2. sign _____        5. debt _____        8. weigh _____

3. edge _____        6. knot _____        9. midget _____

**EXERCISE 9**   Write *one* missing silent letter in the blank space for each word. Many of these examples do not follow the rules above, so use a dictionary to help you, as needed.

1. ____ sychology: the study of the mind

2. ans ____ er: what you give in response to a question

3. ____ nowledge: what you hope to gain in your studies

4. bri ____ ge: something you use to cross a river

5. forei ____ n: from another country

6. bom ____ : something that explodes

7. ____ onest: truthful

8. ____ hole: entire, complete

9. recei ____ t: a piece of paper proving you bought something

10. windo ____ : something you look through

11. pe ____ ple: the plural of person

12. colum ____ : a row of something

13. c ____ romosome: a genetic unit

14. g ____ ess: what you do when you're not sure

15. i ____ land: a piece of land surrounded by water

16. lis ____ en: hear

**EXERCISE 10**   As in Exercise 9, fill in each blank with one silent letter.

1. wa___l___k: travel by foot

2. clim__b__: go up a mountain

3. __p__neumonia: a respiratory illness

4. __w__rite: use a pen on paper

5. sno__w__: cold white substance

6. ta___l___k: speak

7. fas__t__en: what you do with your seatbelt

8. plum__b__er: person who works with sinks and pipes

9. cou___l___d: past tense of "can"

10. of__t__en: more than sometimes

11. We__d__nesday: after Tuesday

12. mus__c__le: what you get from lifting weights

13. bus__i__ness: store, company, etc.

14. lam__b__: young sheep

15. __h__our: sixty minutes

16. mor__t__gage: loan for a house

17. Illinoi__s__: state in the Midwest

**EXERCISE 11**   Listen and write as your instructor reads sentences containing words with silent letters. You will hear each sentence three times.

*Online Teaching Center*

1. _____

2. _____

3. _____

4. _____

5. _____

6. _____

7. _____

8. _____

9. _____

10. _____

## C. CAPITALIZATION OF WORDS IN TITLES OF BOOKS, ARTICLES, AND OTHER WRITTEN WORK

There is some difference in opinion as to which words in titles should begin with capital letters. Here, however, are some rules that cover common usage and that may be accepted by many schools, professional organizations, and employers. You may use these rules for your own writing, such as when you compose titles for your compositions and other papers.

### Capitalization of Words in Titles Rules

Capitalize all nouns, pronouns, verbs, adjectives, and adverbs.

> **Examples:**   The *Big Ship Sails Slowly*
>
> It's *Yours* at Last

Capitalize prepositions only when they are stressed.

> **Examples:**   Brush *Up On* English
>
> The Man *from* Philadelphia

Capitalize the first and last words.

> **Example:**   *A* City to Travel *To*

Capitalize the first word after a colon (:).

> **Example:**   Chicago: *The* Windy City

Capitalize only the first part of a hyphenated (-) word.

> **Example:**   New Developments in *E-mail*

Use lowercase letters for all other words.

---

**EXERCISE 12**

Rewrite the following titles, using capital letters where necessary. Refer to the rules above for assistance.

1. retire at sixty-three

   _____

2. computers in the workplace

   _____

3. a drive through the wine region

   _____

4. a history of biochemistry

   _____

5. turn on your creativity

   _____

6. education is the answer

_____

7. words to live by

_____

8. eat for two: a diet for expectant mothers

_____

9. talking about literature

_____

10. young but already successful

_____

11. ten ways to spend a rainy day

_____

12. traveling with children: plan for the unexpected

_____

13. everyday applications of web-based research

_____

14. the new road to financial security

_____

15. art in the ancient world

_____

**EXERCISE 13**  Use your imagination to compose titles for the following items. Be sure to capitalize words when appropriate. Share your titles with your classmates.

1. a book about your life

_____

2. a newspaper article about a classmate's birth/marriage/college graduation/etc.

_____

3. a mystery story

_____

4. a science fiction novel

_____

5. a composition about spelling

_____

6. Your choice:

_____

_Spelling Word Bank_  In the Spelling Word Bank at the end of this book, write words from this chapter that you find especially difficult or interesting or that are especially good examples.

# CHAPTER 4 TEST

## TOTAL = 25 POINTS, 1 POINT EACH ITEM

**A.** Circle the letter of the item that is correctly spelled.

| | | | | |
|---|---|---|---|---|
| 1. a. instructer | b. instructor | 6. a. surprize | b. surprise |
| 2. a. submission | b. submition | 7. a. decition | b. decision |
| 3. a. realize | b. realise | 8. a. adaptasion | b. adaptation |
| 4. a. paralize | b. paralyze | 9. a. assesser | b. assessor |
| 5. a. trainer | b. trainor | 10. a. mechanize | b. mechanise |

**B.** Circle the letter of the correct answer.

1. Which letter is silent in *listen?*

   a. s      b. t

2. Which letter is silent in *knot?*

   a. k      b. n

3. Which letter is silent in *ledge?*

   a. d      b. g

4. Which letter is silent in *island?*

   a. s      b. l

5. Which letter is silent in *where?*

   a. w      b. h

6. Which letter is silent in *skate?*

   a. k      b. e

7. Which letter is silent in *comb?*

   a. m      b. b

8. Which letter is silent in *honest?*

   a. h      b. t

9. Which letter is silent in *sign?*

   a. g      b. n

10. Which letter is silent in *talk?*

    a. l      b. k

11. Which letter is silent in *chemistry?*

    a. c      b. h

12. Which letter is silent in *guitar?*

    a. u      b. i

**C.** Circle the letter of the title that is appropriately capitalized.

1. a. Jefferson: a Man of Many Talents

   b. Jefferson: A Man of Many Talents

2. a. A Two-Month Course in Greek Grammar

   b. A Two-month Course in Greek Grammar

3. a. Dreams to Live for

   b. Dreams to Live For

## A. COMMON ADJECTIVE SUFFIXES

Whether to add −*able* or −*ible* in forming adjectives is a frequent spelling question. There are many more words that end in −*able* than words that end in −*ible*, so if you must guess, use −*able*. Also, here are a few guidelines to help you decide.

*valuable*          *edible*

## Adding −*able* and −*ible* Rules

In general, you can add −*able* to a root that is a complete word.

**comfort** (complete word) **+ able = comfortable**

If the root is a complete word that ends in *e*, drop the *e* and add −*able*.

**value** (complete word ending in *e*) **+ able = valuable**

But keep the *e* if the final sound is *s* or *j*.

**place** (final sound *s*) **+ able = placeable**

**change** (final sound *j*) **+ able = changeable**

If the root is a complete word that ends in consonant + *y*, change the *y* to *i* and add −*able*.

**rely + able = reliable**

If the root is not a complete word, add −*ible*.

**poss** (not a complete word) **+ ible = possible**

However, there are many exceptions to these rules, such as

**separable** ("separ" is not a complete word) **and reproducible** ("reproduce" is a complete word)

**EXERCISE 1**   Follow the rules above to add −*able* or −*ible* to each of the roots. There are no exceptions to the rules in this exercise. Write the new words in the spaces provided.

1. elig _____

2. knowledge _____

3. depend _____

4. remark _____

5. trace _____

6. incred _____

7. aud _____

8. fashion _____

9. terr _____

10. admire _____

11. divis _____

12. intellig _____

13. like _____

14. break _____

15. manage _____

16. horr _____

17. consider _____

18. move _____

19. accept _____

20. vis _____

21. suit _____

22. adore _____

23. adapt _____

24. notice _____

25. unthink _____

26. ed _____

**EXERCISE 2**   These words are all exceptions. Add −*able* or −*ible* by **not** following the rules in the chart. That is, add −*able* to roots that are not complete words and add −*ible* to roots that are complete words. Write the new words in the spaces provided.

1. response _____

2. flex _____

3. inevit _____

4. combust _____

5. access _____

6. irrit _____

7. digest _____

8. applic _____

9. force _____

10. cap _____

**EXERCISE 3**   Answer each question by writing an appropriate −*able*/−*ible* adjective from Exercises 1 and 2. There is more than one appropriate response in some cases.

What word describes...

1. ...someone who is popular with everyone? _____

2. ...someone who has read and studied a lot? _____

3. ...something that is very, very bad? _____

4. ...something that we can't imagine? _____

5. ...someone whom we can always count on? _____

6. ...something that is very delicate? _____

7. ...something that we can hear? _____

8. ...something that we can see? _____

9. ...something that we can eat? _____

10. ...something that is appropriate? _____

11. ...someone who always has the latest clothes? _____

12. ...something that we can understand? _____

13. ...someone who qualifies for something? _____

14. ...someone whom we consider a role model? _____

15. ...something that will happen no matter what we do? _____

16. ...something that burns easily? _____

17. ...someone who changes easily? _____

18. ...something that is unusual? _____

19. ...someone who is very cute? _____

20. ...someone who is in a bad mood? _____

21. ...something that can be separated into smaller parts? _____

22. ...something that is available to everyone? _____

23. ...something that can change locations? _____

24. ...something that we see and think about? _____

25. ...something that we can find if we look carefully? _____

Other suffixes used to form adjectives are —*ous* and —*ious*.

*poisonous*

*delicious*

# Adding *—ous* and *—ious* Rules

Add *—ous* to most roots.

**poison + ous = poisonous**

Drop the *e* from a root that ends in a silent *e*.

**fame + ous = famous**

But keep the silent *e* if the last consonant sound in the root is *j*.

**gorge** (ends with a *j* sound) **+ ous = gorgeous**

If a root ends in consonant + *y*, change the *y* to *i* and add *—ous*.

**glory + ous = glorious**

When the last consonant sound in the root is s or *t*, add *—ious*. The suffix will begin with the *sh* sound.

**delic + ious = delicious**

**caut + ious = cautious**

Learn these common exceptions:

**curious, previous**

**EXERCISE 4**    Add *—ous* or *—ious* to each of the roots to create new words.

1. grace _____

2. nerve _____

3. outrage _____

4. danger _____

5. mountain _____

6. infect _____

7. mystery _____

8. gener _____

9. advantage _____

10. nutrit      _____

11. caut        _____

12. superstit   _____

13. joy         _____

14. prec        _____

15. consc       _____

16. monoton     _____

17. suspic      _____

18. courage     _____

19. ambit       _____

20. fame        _____

21. murder      _____

22. poison      _____

23. melody      _____

24. delic       _____

25. harmony     _____

26. marvel      _____

**EXERCISE 5**  Write original sentences with adjectives ending in −*ous* and −*ious*. Try to use more than one adjective in each sentence. Ask a classmate to read and comment on your sentences.

1. _____

2. _____

3. _____

4. _____

5. _____

6. _____

7. _____

8. _____

9. _____

10. _____

## B. IRREGULAR PLURALS

one *leaf*—two *leaves*

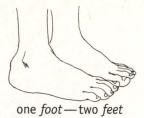

one *foot*—two *feet*

Regular plurals in English are formed by adding *—s*. Early in your study of the English language, you also encountered irregular plurals, such as *leaf—leaves, foot—feet,* and *woman—women.*

**EXERCISE 6**

See how many of the common irregular forms you remember by writing the plurals of the nouns in the spaces provided. Use a dictionary to check your spelling, as needed.

1. mouse _____
2. child _____
3. foot _____
4. wife _____
5. person _____
6. life _____
7. deer _____

8. fish _____
9. sheep _____
10. man _____
11. goose _____
12. leaf _____
13. tooth _____
14. self _____

There are other irregular plurals that occur mainly in academic, technical, and formal written English. In the box, some of the most frequent are grouped according to spelling patterns.

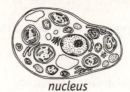
*nucleus*

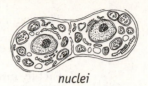
*nuclei*

# Spelling Patterns for Irregular Academic Plurals

| singular (and meaning) | **plural** |
|---|---|
| | **UM → A** |
| medi*um* (means of communication, such as radio or TV) | medi*a* |
| curricul*um* (group of courses in a field of study) | curricul*a* |
| dat*um* (fact) | dat*a* |
| bacteri*um* (microorganism) | bacteri*a* |
| | **ON → A** |
| criteri*on* (standard on which a decision is based) | criteri*a* |
| phenomen*on* (occurrence) | phenomen*a* |
| | **US → I** |
| syllab*us* (written outline or plan for a course) | syllab*i* |
| stimul*us* (something that causes a response) | stimul*i* |
| alumn*us* (a male graduate of a school) | alumn*i* (male or mixed group) |
| nucle*us* (central part of something) | nucle*i* |
| | **A → AE** |
| alumn*a* (a female graduate of a school) | alumn*ae* |
| | **IS → ES** |
| cris*is* (unstable condition) | cris*es* |
| thes*is* (research document required for a degree) | thes*es* |
| hypothes*is* (explanation to be tested) | hypothes*es* |
| analys*is* (study of the parts of something) | analys*es* |
| | **IX/EX → ICES** |
| append*ix* (supplementary material at the end of a book) | append*ices* |
| ind*ex* (alphabetized list of subjects in a book) | ind*ices* |

*Note: A few nouns in this category also have regular plural forms. For example, syllabi/ syllabuses, appendices/appendixes, and indices/indexes are all correct. Consult a dictionary if you would like to know which nouns have acceptable regular plural forms.*

**EXERCISE 7**   Add the endings necessary to complete each word in the correct form for the context, singular or plural. Refer to the patterns above as needed.

1. The most important criteri_____ for the judging of the art show is creativity.

2. The scientists wanted to test several hypothes_____ during the experiment.

3. The scholarship was funded by an alumn_____/alumn_____ of the university.

4. It is the responsibility of instructors to develop syllab_____ for their courses. Faculty must also develop curricul_____ for their programs.

5. The politician complained that the medi_____ were not reporting his activities in a positive way.

6. Please refer to the append_____ of irregular verbs in the back of your book.

7. Serious unemployment and hunger are among the cris_____ that country is facing.

8. More dat_____ are needed to make a decision about the business plan.

9. Hurricanes and tornadoes are weather phenomen_____ that cause great damage each year.

10. The goal to earn more money can be the stimul_____ students need to finish college.

11. We are exposed to many bacteri_____ in our daily lives.

12. A master's thes_____ is a requirement of many graduate programs.

13. The experts' analys_____ of the evidence at the crime scene differed greatly from each other.

14. To find a fact in a book, you may check the ind_____ to see if a page number is listed there.

15. Washington, D.C. is the nucle_____ of the United States government.

**EXERCISE 8**   Based on the examples in the chart and exercise above, predict the irregular plural forms of the following singular nouns and write them in the spaces provided.

1. empha_____          7. alga _____
2. octopus _____       8. radius _____
3. matrix _____        9. memorandum _____
4. oasis_____          10. vertebra _____
5. automaton _____     11. cactus _____
6. fungus_____         12. diagnosis _____

**EXERCISE 9** | Write ten original sentences, each with a singular or plural form from Exercises 7 and 8.

1. _____

2. _____

3. _____

4. _____

5. _____

6. _____

7. _____

8. _____

9. _____

10. _____

## C. MORE USES OF CAPITAL LETTERS

### Capitalized Words

Degrees, Awards, and Competitions: **Bachelor of Arts in English, the Pulitzer Prize, the Wimbledon Championships**

Businesses, schools, and organizations: **South Community Bank, the University of North Carolina, the Rockefeller Foundation**

Brand names: **Ford cars, Hewlett-Packard computers**

*Note: In the exercises that follow, remember to also capitalize the first letters of categories of words introduced in Chapter 2: geographical areas and features, languages, nationalities, ethnicities, holidays, days of the week, and months. Refer to Chapter 2 as needed.*

**EXERCISE 10**

Proofread the paragraph for lowercase letters that should be capitals. When you find an error, cross out the lowercase letter, and write a capital letter above it.

César Chávez (1927–1993) was a mexican-american civil rights and labor leader who was born in arizona and raised in a family of migrant farm workers. As a boy, Chávez completed only the eighth grade, but his lifelong dedication to reading and study made him a well-read and educated man. After a tour of duty in the u.s. navy, Chávez returned to california, married, and began working as an organizer for the community services organization, a latino civil rights group. In 1962, he founded the national farm workers association, which later became the united farm workers. Leading strikes and boycotts against such products as the wine of e. & j. gallo and the lettuce of bud antle were among Chávez's nonviolent tactics. During his career, he helped hundreds of thousands of farm workers achieve better pay and benefits as well as other rights and protections. After his death in april 1993, family and friends established the César E. Chávez foundation, a nonprofit organization. In 1994, Chávez was awarded the presidential medal of freedom by President Bill Clinton. In 2000, california created a paid state holiday in his honor, César Chávez day, and in 2004, he appeared on a u.s. postage stamp. In numerous cities, including san francisco, houston, milwaukee, and phoenix, schools or streets have been named for him. For many americans, César Chávez is a hero and an inspiration.

**EXERCISE 11**

Respond to the questions with words beginning with capital letters.

1. Do you have or want a college degree? What is it?

   _____

2. Have you ever received an award? What was it?

   _____

3. Imagine you are to present awards to several of your classmates. Who are the students and what are the names of the awards?

   Student                          Award

   _____        _____

   _____        _____

   _____        _____

4. a) What school do you currently attend?

   _____

   b) What schools did you attend in the past?

   _____

5. What businesses do you often visit...

   a) ...to buy food or to eat?

   _____

   _____

   b) ...to buy shoes or clothes?

   _____

   _____

   c) ...to buy electronics, music, etc.?

   _____

   _____

   d) your choice:

   _____

   _____

6. What brands do you like or own in the following categories?

   a) computers:

   _____

   b) cars:

   _____

   c) watches:

   _____

   d) blue jeans:

   _____

   e) your choice:

   _____

7. What organizations do you belong to or have you belonged to in the past?

_____

8. What social, educational, or charitable organizations do you know of in your community?

_____

**EXERCISE 12**     Rewrite the sentences, changing lowercase letters to capital letters where appropriate.

1. Bill Gates, who was born in seattle, washington in october 1955, dropped out of harvard university to found his company, microsoft.

_____

_____

_____

2. Julia Child (1912–2004), one of america's most famous chefs, studied at le cordon bleu, a cooking school in paris, and starred in a number of TV programs that taught viewers to prepare french food.

_____

_____

_____

3. Hannibal, a general from the ancient city of carthage, is famous for leading his army on a dangerous march from spain through the pyrenees and the alps to italy in 218 BC.

_____

_____

_____

4. Marie Sklodowska Curie, a polish scientist, was awarded the nobel prize in chemistry in 1911 and spent her later years working at the radium institute, an organization dedicated to improving the human condition.

_____

_____

_____

5. Most of us are familiar with ikea, sony, and mercedes-benz, which are just a few of the foreign brands available in north america.

_____

_____

_____

***Spelling Word Bank***   In the Spelling Word Bank at the end of this book, write words from this chapter that you find especially difficult or interesting or that are especially good examples.

# CHAPTER 5 TEST

## TOTAL = 25 POINTS, 1 POINT FOR EACH ITEM

**A.** Circle the letter of the item that is correctly spelled.

1. a. responsable    b. responsible     6. a. honorable    b. honorible

2. a. nutritous    b. nutritious     7. a. couragous    b. courageous

3. a. furious    b. furyous     8. a. changable    b. changeable

4. a. horrable    b. horrible     9. a. conscous    b. conscious

5. a. lovable    b. loveable     10. a. nervous    b. nerveous

**B.** Circle the letter of the item that is the appropriate plural form.

1. a. shelfs    b. shelves     6. a. nucleuses    b. nuclei

2. a. media    b. medii     7. a. women    b. womens

3. a. deer    b. deeren     8. a. bacteria    b. bacterium

4. a. diagnoces    b. diagnoses     9. a. teeth    b. teethes

5. a. alumnus    b. alumni     10. a. phenomena    b. phenomenon

**C.** Find and correct the words that should begin with capital letters. Cross out the lowercase letters, and write capital letters above them. You will need a total of twenty-five capital letters.

1. After receiving a master of arts in sociology, she continued her studies at notre dame university.

2. In 1999, the nobel peace prize was awarded to an organization, doctors without borders.

3. In the u.s., japanese cars manufactured by toyota, honda, and nissan are very popular.

4. At the end of the nineteenth century, mail-order catalog companies such as sears, roebuck and co. and montgomery ward became very well known.

5. The world cup, an international soccer championship, is the world's most popular sporting event.

# REVIEW OF CHAPTERS 2 – 5

**EXERCISE 1**

Write new words by adding the suffixes indicated. Follow the rules for doubling consonants, dropping the *e*, changing *y* to *i*, and adding −*s* and −*es*, which you studied in Chapters 2 and 3.

1. spot + ed _____
2. offer + ing _____
3. insure + ance _____
4. market + ing _____
5. thirsty + er _____
6. library + s _____
7. cross + s _____
8. worry + ed _____
9. manage + ment _____
10. pursue + ing _____
11. century + s _____
12. clap + ed _____
13. interpret + ed _____
14. noisy + ly _____
15. do + s _____
16. annoy + ance _____
17. obey + ed _____
18. friendly + est _____
19. stay + s _____
20. remove + al _____
21. fog + y _____
22. shower + ed _____
23. fly + ing _____
24. control + ing _____

**EXERCISE 2**

Proofread the paragraphs for errors in doubling consonants, dropping the *e*, changing *y* to *i*, and adding −*s* and −*es*. Follow the rules you studied in Chapters 2 and 3.

1. Although soccer is the world's most popular sport, it hasn't enjoied the same success in the United States, where Americans are busyly plaing their traditional favorites, baseball, football, and basketball. However, that picture is slowly changeing. Immigrants are bringing soccer along with their languages and cultures, and city parks are often the settings for evenning and weekend matchs. Also, satellite TV broadcasts soccer games from foreign countrys, permiting viewers to learn about the sport in their own liveing rooms. Moreover, soccer is becomming part of many school athletic programs, so children are studing and practicing the sport at young ages. Parents themselfs are taking an interest as they see their children runing about on soccer fields. As the U.S. watchs and learnes about soccer, we can expect to see more of it in the future.

2. Makeing your own soup is not too complicated, and the product is much tastyer and more satisfing than anything from cans or boxs. In preparing homemade soup, shoping does involve refering to a list, and choping vegetables and stiring the soup do take time and attention—but perhaps not as much as you might think. All of the world's cultures have traditional soups that you can try by fixxing them in your own kitchen. You can make recipes your own by ading more of the ingredients you like and fewwer of those you don't. You can make large quantitys, and once your soup is ready, you have the option of freezeing some of it for later use or eatting it all in a few days. Next time you're hungry, think about cookking some soup. Use your bigest pot, the easiest recipe, and your imagineation to make an absolutly wonderful meal.

**EXERCISE 3**

*Online Teaching Center*

Review the names of the letters of the alphabet. Then, listen and write the words as your instructor spells them. You will hear each word spelled twice.

1. _____       7. _____

2. _____       8. _____

3. _____       9. _____

4. _____      10. _____

5. _____      11. _____

6. _____      12. _____

**EXERCISE 4**

Proofread the paragraphs, inserting and crossing out apostrophes as needed. Also, correct errors with possessive adjectives. Follow the guidelines you studied in Chapter 3.

1. Although the city has raised it's taxes by two percent, it hasn't made a difference in the fire departments budget. That department estimates that 100 additional firefighters are needed to ensure the safety of the citys two million resident's. According to the fire commissioners report, if more firefighters are'nt hired, the city wo'nt be able to respond to all of its emergencies.

2. Colleges and universities should consider the needs of they're students in developing program's and courses. In order to determine the student's needs, it's often necessary to conduct surveys or opinion polls that ask students about their preferences. For example, many student's might indicate that they'd be interested in online coursework or in weekend classes. Schools that do'nt take student's wishes into account may lose enrollment to schools who's students are invited to express their needs.

*sun*

*son*

**EXERCISE 5**    Put the letters in the correct order to write pairs of homonyms that you studied in Chapter 3. Look at the words in Chapter 3 if you have difficulty with this exercise.

1. uleb/wbel            _____/_____

2. rehe/eahr            _____/_____

3. cepie/eapec          _____/_____

4. wrehe/reaw           _____/_____

5. grohtuh/ehtwr        _____/_____

6. rebak/rebak          _____/_____

7. repa/ripa            _____/_____

8. etsi/thigs           _____/_____

9. nosels/selsen        _____/_____

10. roulf/worfel        _____/_____

11. seon/koswn          _____/_____

12. trewahe/threweh     _____/_____

13. lowud/dowo          _____/_____

14. elam/ilam           _____/_____

*teacher/instructor/professor*

**EXERCISE 6**   Rewrite the words, adding −*er* and −*or* to the roots. Apply the rules that were presented in Chapter 4.

1. rob _____     7. spectate _____

2. invest _____     8. bet _____

3. murder _____     9. sing _____

4. credit _____     10. alternate _____

5. clean _____     11. lend _____

6. office _____     12. borrow _____

**EXERCISE 7**   Rewrite the words, adding −*ion* by following the rules you studied in Chapter 4.

1. collaborate _____     9. commit _____

2. donate _____     10. persuade _____

3. invent _____     11. expand _____

4. complete _____     12. combine _____

5. supervise _____     13. conclude _____

6. profess _____     14. converse _____

7. create _____     15. comprehend _____

8. provide _____     16. invite _____

**EXERCISE 8** Rewrite the roots adding −ize, −ise, or −yze by following the examples you studied in Chapter 4.

1. superv _____  8. comprom _____

2. recogn _____  9. criminal _____

3. surpr _____  10. rev _____

4. real _____  11. maxim _____

5. civil _____  12. exerc _____

6. paral _____  13. anal _____

7. modern _____  14. advert _____

**EXERCISE 9** Fill in the missing silent letters as in Chapter 4.

1. cas _____ le: home of a princess

2. ri _____ _____ t: opposite of *wrong*

3. c _____ aracter: personality

4. sof _____ en: make less hard

5. Arkansa _____: state near Missouri

6. thou _____ _____ t: past of *think*

7. ba _____ ge: a police officer wears one

8. _____ nife: a cutting tool

9. dum _____: not smart

10. follo _____: opposite of *lead*

11. b _____ ild: construct

12. min _____: belonging to me

13. fu _____ ge: chocolate candy

14. _____ sychiatrist: doctor of the mind

15. shou _____ d: ought to

16. nei _____ _____ bor: person next door

17. cha _____ k: white substance

18. w _____ y: question word

**EXERCISE 10**  Proofread the reading selection, changing lowercase to capital letters as needed. Use capital letters as presented in Chapters 2, 4, and 5.

Jane Goodall, born in london in 1934, is a british primatologist who conducted a forty-year study of chimpanzees in gombe national park in tanzania. She lived in the jungle among the animals, who grew to trust her. Her research demonstrated, among other things, that chimpanzees use tools, a discovery that has changed scientific thinking about nonhuman animals. Two of her books, *my friends the wild chimpanzees* and *in the shadow of man*, became quite popular and introduced her ideas and work to the general public.

Goodall had been interested in animals since her early childhood and financed her own first trip to africa. In 1957, she was hired as a secretary by anthropologist Louis Leakey, who was working in kenya, and she began studying chimpanzees in 1960. However, she had no formal scientific training. She returned to england and earned a ph.d. in ethology from cambridge university in 1964. Then, she went back to her research. Her work revealed that chimpanzees have individual personalities, close family relationships, and many other "human" qualities. In 2000, her life's work was summed up in photographs in *Jane Goodall: 40 years at gombe.* She is also the author of many academic publications as well as a number of books for children.

In 1977, Dr. Goodall established the Jane Goodall institute, which is based in arlington, virginia, and which furthers research and leads efforts to protect chimpanzees and all living things and their habitats. Today, she devotes most of her time to writing, speaking, and teaching about animal and environmental issues. She has been honored with awards from many countries, including the medal of tanzania, japan's kyoto prize, the benjamin franklin medal in life science, and the gandhi/king award for nonviolence. She has also received honorary degrees from numerous institutions, including utrecht university in the netherlands, stirling university in scotland, providence university in taiwan, and ludwig-maximilians university in germany. In 2002, she was appointed a united nations "messenger of peace," and in february 2004, she was named a dame of the british empire. Jane Goodall is recognized around the world for her message of hope and her belief that individuals can make a difference.

**EXERCISE 11**  Rewrite the roots, adding −*able* or −*ible* according to the rules in Chapter 5.

1. tax _____

2. enjoy _____

3. favor _____

4. permiss _____

5. argue _____

6. excuse _____

7. compat _____

8. envy _____

9. disagree _____

10. honor _____

11. cred _____

12. forget _____

**EXERCISE 12**  Rewrite the roots, adding −*ous* or −*ious* according to the rules in Chapter 5.

1. glamor _____

2. fury _____

3. enorm _____

4. anx _____

5. ceremony _____

6. space _____

7. ridicule _____

8. envy _____

9. odor _____

10. study _____

11. adventure _____

12. courage _____

**EXERCISE 13**    Fill in the chart with the missing singular and irregular plural forms of the nouns, following the examples presented in Chapter 5.

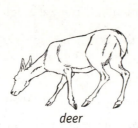

*deer*

*deer*

| SINGULAR | PLURAL | SINGULAR | PLURAL |
|---|---|---|---|
| leaf | | | people |
| | teeth | | sheep |
| woman | | mouse | |
| | lives | self | |
| | men | | children |
| deer | | | fish |
| foot | | goose | |
| | bacteria | phenomenon | |
| nucleus | | | analyses |
| index | | crisis | |
| | oases | curriculum | |
| datum | | alga | |
| octopus | | | media |
| | theses | stimulus | |
| vertebra | | alumna | |
| | hypotheses | criterion | |
| radius | | memorandum | |
| | diagnoses | | cacti |
| | fungi | | appendices |

**EXERCISE 14**

Proofread the items, crossing out all errors of types presented in Chapters 2–5. Write the correct spelling above the errors.

1. After sleeping for nine hours, we felt relaxxed and comfortible and completely ready to work again.

2. The Smith's three childrens attend george washington high school.

3. The dutys of a lifeguard at the beach include rescueing swimers who get into trouble.

 4. The american writer Edgar Allan Poe was born on january 19, 1809, in boston, massachusetts. He is best known for his poetry, especially "the raven," and his short stories, which include "the black cat" and "the murders in the rue morgue." He is generally regarded as the creater of the detective story. Poe died in baltimore, maryland, in october 1849, in mysteryous circumstances, imitating many of his fameous works.

5. The american red cross recommends the following first aid for animal bites: Wash the wound with soap under runing water, and apply antibiotic ointment and dressing.

6. The Inca city of machu picchu, high in the andes mountains of peru at an elevation of around eight thousand foots, was added to the world heritage list by the united nations educational, scientific, and cultural organizeation (UNESCO) in 1983. The city, which is hauntingly beautyful, was abandonned about five hundred years ago and was never discoverred by the spanish who conquered peru. Currently, machu picchu draws over 500,000 visitters a year.

7. The word *sandwich* comes from the name of the inventer of the food, the Earl of Sandwich, a well-known british gambler of the eighteenth century. While gambling, the Earl disliked stoping to eat, so he ordered slices of meat and cheese served between peaces of bread. In that way, he could eat with one hand while continueing his games. Today, sandwichs are very popular, and many people eat them while their driving, studing, or watching television.

8. A celebrateion of relatively recent origin, father's day did'nt become an official holiday in the united states until 1966. It falls on the third sunday in june. In contrast, mother's day has been officially celebrated on the second sunday in may since 1914.

**EXERCISE 15**    As in Exercise 14, proofread the items, crossing out all errors of types presented in Chapters 2–5. Write the correct spelling above the errors.

1. We were furyous with our cousin over his terrable behavior. It was inexcusible.

2. Grocery list:

   2 cans of tomatos                    2 bunchs of bananas

   1 pound of cherrys                   2 loafs of bread

   2 boxs of cereal                     10 pounds of potatos

   1 bag of frozen french frys          6 peachs

   1 bag of dryed mushrooms             1 carton of whiping cream

3. The flags of the worlds' nations are fascinateing to see and study. We can immediately note many similaritys among them. For example, certain color combinasions are very common. australia, the czech republic, the dominican republic, france, laos, norway, the united states and many others have red, white, and blue flags. Red, white, and green is also a popular color scheme. italy, iran, mexico, and tajikistan are among the countrys who's flags are those colors. Another similarity can be seen in symbols. The flags of cameroon, honduras, new zealand, and syria feature stars; malaysias', pakistans', tunisias', and turkeys' flags feature crescent moons. denmark, greece, sweden, and Switzerland have crosses on they're flags.

4. Jupiter is the bigest planet in our solar system. It's mass is more than two times the mass of all the other planets together. It's diameter is eleven times that of the Earth, but, surprizingly, it rotates so rapidly that it's day is less than ten Earth hours long. It has enormious thunderstorms, and it also has volcanos that are much hoter than those on Earth. Jupiter has at least sixty-one moons, some of which are visable threw binoculars.

5. The yo-yo was first used as a toy by the chinese several thousand years ago. It was made of ivory and had a silk cord. However, the word *yo-yo* is'nt chinese. It comes from the tagalog language of the philippines. There, the yo-yo was'nt a toy. It was much larger, made of would, and was used as a weapon in hunting. A huntor threw the yo-yo, and it wraped itself around the legs of an animal, bringing it to the ground.

6. The district of columbia isn't a state and it isn't a city, but it contains and is the same size as the city of washington, our national capital. In 1790, philadelphia was chosen as a temporary ten-year capital. The sight for the permanent capital on the banks of the potomac river was chosen by President George Washington in october 1790. The land was sold to the government by citizens in the states of maryland and virginia, and construcsion began that year. In 1800, President John Adams moved to washington, and it became the official capital. Incredably, residents of the district of columbia could'nt vote in presidential elections until 1961, and they were'nt allowed to elect their own mayor until 1974.

***Spelling Word Bank***    In the Spelling Word Bank at the end of this book, write words from this review section that you find especially difficult or interesting or that are especially good examples.

# CHAPTER 6

## A. COMMON NEGATIVE PREFIXES

In the English language, there are a number of negative prefixes that can be added at the beginning of words to change their meanings. There are a few rules to help you decide which prefix might be used with a word. The following negative prefixes are used with nouns, adjectives, and adverbs. All of them mean "not."

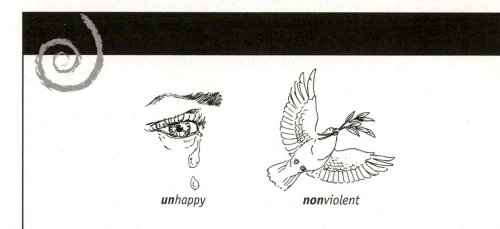

*un*happy                    *non*violent

### Rules for Forming Words with Negative Prefixes

*il-* is added to words beginning with *l*, as in **illegal.** Note that there are two *ll*'s in the word.

*ir-* is added to words beginning with *r*, as in **irregular.** Again, note the double consonant (*rr*).

*im-* is added to words beginning with *m*, *p*, or *b*, as in **immature** (with two *m*'s), **impossible**, and **imbalance.**

Exceptions: There are many exceptions to the rules. For example, **unpopular, unlucky,** and **unreliable** are correct forms. (*Impopular, illucky,* and *irreliable* are not correct.)

**EXERCISE 1**   Rewrite each word, adding *il-, ir-,* and *im-* by applying the rules. The rules apply in all of these cases.

1. polite          _____          8. responsible      _____

2. logical         _____          9. perfect          _____

3. reversible      _____          10. proper          _____

4. legible         _____          11. mature          _____

5. replaceable     _____          12. legitimate      _____

6. moral           _____          13. regular         _____

7. legal           _____          14. modest          _____

**EXERCISE 2**   Fill in the blanks by adding the negative prefixes below to the words in *italics.* Remember that some words will have double consonants. Note that *dis-* is the only prefix below that may be used with verbs, in addition to nouns, adjectives, and adverbs. In most cases, there are no rules, so you may consult your instructor, classmates, or dictionary, as needed.

un-    il-    im-    ir-    in-    non-    dis-

1. Drinks that are not *alcoholic* are referred to as _____.

2. People who are not *employed* are _____.

3. Our world is not *perfect*—it is _____.

4. When we do not *agree,* we _____.

5. Many countries that were *dependent* on colonial powers in the past are now _____.

6. With age, documents can become _____. They are so damaged that they are not *legible* and cannot be read.

7. Children often do not *like* certain foods. For example, spinach is a vegetable that many children _____.

8. The prices of cars are sometimes *negotiable,* but prices in a department store are almost always _____.

9. The instructor's attempts to explain the concept were not *successful.* They were _____.

10. In general, criminals are not *honest.* They are _____.

11. In the United States, there are adults who cannot read or write. They are not *literate*; they are _____.

12. Although we like to think our lives are *predictable,* and we know what will happen, sometimes our lives can be very _____.

13. Talking on a cell phone in class or in a theater is not *appropriate*. It is _____ behavior.

14. Race and ethnicity should not be *relevant* in hiring decisions. They are _____.

15. We booked a flight from Chicago to Mexico City that did not *stop* in any other cities. It was a _____ flight.

16. His long explanation was not *necessary*. It was _____.

17. The answer was not *correct*. It was _____.

**EXERCISE 3**

Below, make a list of additional words you know that have the negative prefixes you studied in this section. Share your list with a classmate, and ask him or her to check your spelling. Add the words on his or her list to your own list.

*dis-*                    *non-*                    *il-*




*im-*                     *ir-*                     *in-*




*un-*

## B. COMMONLY CONFUSED PAIRS OF WORDS

*desert*                    *dessert*

There are many pairs of words that are easily confused because their spellings are similar; however, their meanings are different, and usually, their pronunciations are different, too. In the pair above, one word has a single *s*, and the other has a double *ss*. Also, **des ert** is stressed on the first syllable, while **des sert** is stressed on the second syllable. Practice pronouncing them to hear the difference.

**EXERCISE 4**     Study these word pairs and their meanings in parentheses ( ).

| | | |
|---|---|---|
| 1. | **advice** (suggestion about what to do) | **advise** (give advice) |
| 2. | **angel** (being from heaven) | **angle** (where two straight lines meet) |
| 3. | **assure** (promise) | **ensure** (make sure) |
| 4. | **complement** (be a good addition to) | **compliment** (express praise or admiration) |
| 5. | **desert** (a dry place) | **dessert** (sweet dish after a meal) |
| 6. | **emigrate** (leave one country for another) | **immigrate** (enter a new country to live) |
| 7. | **eminent** (well known and respected) | **imminent** (ready to happen soon) |
| 8. | **lay** (put or place something somewhere) | **lie** (rest in a horizontal position) |
| 9. | **quiet** (not noisy) | **quite** (very) |
| 10. | **rise** (move upwards) | **raise** (lift something up) |
| 11. | **thorough** (complete) | **through** (in one side and out the other) |

Now fill in the blanks with words from the chart. The numbers in the chart correspond to the numbers of the items below. You will use each word once.

1. a. Most of us rely on the _____ of our friends and family when we have problems.

   b. It is the responsibility of a college's faculty to _____ students on what courses to take.

2. a. Although the child is not well behaved, his grandmother refers to him as "my little _____."

   b. The wall and floor come together to form a 90-degree _____.

3. a. I _____ you I will meet you first thing tomorrow morning.

   b. You should always lock your car to _____ that it isn't stolen.

4. a. A green salad is a typical _____ to many American meals.

   b. It's polite to _____ your host on the food you are served.

5. a. If you want to lose weight, you can give up eating _____.

   b. The Sahara is a large _____ in Africa.

6. a. People from all over the world _____ to the United States.

   b. Because the economy of their country was so poor, many people decided to _____.

7. a. Relations between the countries were very bad, and we feared that war was _____.

   b. Albert Einstein was an _____ scientist of the twentieth century.

8. a. You may _____ your completed homework papers on the instructor's desk.

   b. If you have a headache, _____ down and close your eyes for a few minutes.

9. a. We are expected to be _____ in libraries and hospitals.

   b. It is usually _____ cold in Canada in winter.

10. a. Does the sun _____ in the east or the west?

    b. It's appropriate to _____ your hand when you want to say something in a large meeting or class.

11. a. I walked _____ the park on my way home.

    b. The accountant conducted a very _____ review of the company's finances.

**EXERCISE 5**    Study these pairs of words and note their different meanings.

| 1.  | **accept** (approve) | **except** (not including) |
|-----|----------------------|----------------------------|
| 2.  | **adapt** (change) | **adopt** (take legal responsibility for) |
| 3.  | **affect** (verb: influence) | **effect** (noun: result) |
| 4.  | **conscience** (feeling of right and wrong) | **conscious** (awake or aware) |
| 5.  | **costume** (special clothes) | **custom** (way of behaving) |
| 6.  | **council** (group of advisors) | **counsel** (give advice) |
| 7.  | **expand** (grow or make larger) | **expend** (use time, money, etc.) |
| 8.  | **farther** (comparative of *far*) | **further** (more, additional) |
| 9.  | **loose** (opposite of *tight*) | **lose** (opposite of *win* and *find*) |
| 10. | **precede** (come before) | **proceed** (to go forward, to continue) |
| 11. | **sit** (rest with bended knees on a chair, etc.) | **set** (put something somewhere) |
| 12. | **than** (word used in comparisons) | **then** (at that time) |

Now fill in each blank space with one of the words from the chart. The numbers in the chart correspond to the numbers of the items below. You will use each word once.

1.  a. I've taken all of the required courses for my degree _____ statistics. I'll take that course next term.

    b. American colleges and universities often _____ courses that students took at foreign institutions.

2.  a. When a person moves to a new country, he or she must _____ to new conditions.

    b. The family decided to _____ a dog from the local animal shelter.

3.  a. Pollution and noise _____ the quality of our lives.

    b. Eating fresh fruit and vegetables can have a good _____ on our health.

4. a. The accident victim was not _____ when the paramedics arrived at the scene.

   b. The killer did not appear to be sorry for his crime. He seemed to have no _____.

5. a. It is the _____ to have a large family meal on Thanksgiving.

   b. A prize was given at the Halloween party for the most imaginative _____.

6. a. The city _____ includes representatives from each of its neighborhoods.

   b. Many schools have employees who _____ students with personal problems.

7. a. The instructor asked the student to _____ his composition by adding details and examples.

   b. In very cold weather, our bodies _____ a lot of energy just to stay warm.

8. a. Which is _____ from Los Angeles? Miami or Houston?

   b. You may call this telephone number for _____ information about the product.

9. a. _____ , light-colored clothes are comfortable in hot weather.

   b. The senator worried that she might _____ the next election.

10. a. Please finish this exercise before you _____ to the next one.

    b. At American meals, the salad will usually _____ the main course.

11. a. I _____ my books on my desk.

    b. In some cultures, it's customary for people to _____ on the floor for meals.

12. a. We'll complete half of the course. _____, we'll take the midterm exam.

    b. Most people agree that good health is more important _____ money.

**EXERCISE 6**    Write the missing letters to form the appropriate words from the charts in Exercises 4 and 5. Try to complete the words before looking at the charts.

1. Chocolate cake is a popular d _____ert.

2. Spring is when people often give their houses a th _____gh cleaning.

3. *L, m,* and *n* pr_____ *o* in the alphabet.

4. A circle is a shape that doesn't have an an _____.

5. His con_____ wouldn't allow him to keep the money he found on the street.

6. The book provides practice to _____ sure that students learn the material.

7. The store bought the building next door in order to ex _____ d its business.

8. Teachers should c_____ ment students when they do good work.

9. Our boss gave us f _____ ther instructions when we needed them.

10. Sea resorts are popular with people who like to l _____ on the beach.

11. That instructor won't _____ cept papers that are more than a week late.

12. The actress who played the queen wore a beautiful c_____ st_____.

13. The students s_____t their homework on the instructor's desk.

14. Sunglasses are easy to l_____s_____, because we put them on and take them off frequently.

15. An accountant can adv_____ you on financial matters.

**EXERCISE 7**   As in Exercise 6, write the missing letters to form the appropriate words from the charts in Exercises 4 and 5. Try to complete the words before looking at the charts.

1. Life in the country is generally more qu _____ than life in the city.

2. The woman's second husband ad _____ ed her children from her first marriage.

3. Death Valley is a hot and dry de _____ rt area in California.

4. The company _____ sured us that the new computer we had ordered would arrive soon.

5. Chocolate is more popular th _____ any other flavor of ice cream.

6. We can see the planet Pluto only th _____ gh a telescope.

7. It is the c _____ st _____ to remove one's shoes before entering a Japanese home.

8. Because the election was _____ inent, the politicians traveled and spoke continuously.

9. One of the reasons the population of the United States increases is because people _____ grate.

10. The committee members waited for their leader before pr ____ c _____ ing with the meeting.

11. I'll see you next week, and I'll tell you my news th _____.

12. You can get adv _____ on how to manage your money from a financial planner or accountant.

13. Charles Dickens, the _____ nent Victorian novelist, wrote *David Copperfield* and *A Tale of Two Cities*.

14. The screw was l _____ se, so I tightened it.

15. The water level in the lake will r _____ se with so much rain.

## C. HYPHENS WITH COMPOUNDS

There is no one set of rules regarding using hyphens (-) in compounds that everyone agrees on. However, in this section, there are rules that many people follow.

*a hand-knit sweater*          *a one-dollar bill*

# Using Hyphens in Compounds

One important use of hyphens (-) is with compounds, two or more words that function as a single unit. Study the following categories, which occur frequently.

### two-word numbers

*21 through 99*:  **thirty-seven, sixty-four,** one hundred **ninety-two,** etc.

*fractions*:  **one-half, three-quarters,** five and **seven-sixteenths,** etc.

*age terms*:  a **four-year-old** house, an **80-year-old** person

**Phrases of two or more words that function as an adjective before a noun, such as,**

> a **ten-pound** bag of rice (number plus noun)
> a **first-class** hotel (ordinal number plus noun)
> a **well-advertised** sale (adverb plus participle)

Exception: Phrases with –*ly* adverbs are not hyphenated.
Examples: An easily understood idea, a highly educated person.

> **high-quality** equipment (adjective plus noun)
> a **user-friendly** system (noun plus adjective)
> **Internet-based** research (noun plus participle)

Note: When nouns function as adjectives, they are not plural. Examples: a **four-year** (not *years*)-old house; a **ten-pound** (not *pounds*) bag of rice

Note: When the phrase is not followed by a noun, no hyphen is used. Examples: The system is **user friendly.** The hotel is **first class.**

**EXERCISE 8** | In the following sentences, insert hyphens in compounds where needed.

1. The restaurant serves Asian influenced food in a friendly atmosphere.

2. Many factory employees earn one and one half times the pay rate when they work extra hours.

3. Modern schools have computer assisted instruction and highly qualified faculty.

4. We paid four thousand fifty three dollars for the hand painted antique.

5. Picasso is a well known name in twentieth century art.

6. Low priced items can be purchased at warehouses and discount stores.

7. Although he's a sixty seven year old man, he has the energy of a thirty year old.

8. Hammers and screwdrivers are frequently used tools. Wrenches are also frequently used.

9. Foreign language dictionaries are available in many big city bookstores.

10. Because he hadn't done it earlier in the term, he had to read a three hundred page book and write a ten page paper, all in a twenty four hour period.

**EXERCISE 9** | Write a hyphenated compound and a noun, such as *ten-minute break* or *better-educated person,* in each blank space. Use the italicized words to help you.

1. The *class* meets for *four hours.* It's a _____.

2. *Professor* Jones is *well respected.* She's a _____.

3. That *student* is in the *third grade.* He's a _____.

4. Many traffic *accidents* are *related* to the use of *alcohol.* They are _____ _____.

5. *Art* that is *generated* by *computers* is popular. It's _____.

6. Many members of the *middle class* live in that *neighborhood.* It's a _____.

7. The *car* cost *twenty thousand dollars.* It's a_____ _____.

8. The *paper* was *half finished.* It was a_____ _____.

9. Delis sell *food* that is *ready to eat.* It's _____.

10. *Restaurants* in many cities are *free* of cigarette *smoke.* They are_____ _____.

***Spelling Word Bank***   In the Spelling Word Bank at the end of this book, write words from this chapter that you find especially difficult or interesting or that are especially good examples.

# CHAPTER 6 TEST

## TOTAL = 25 POINTS, 1 POINT FOR EACH ITEM

**A.** Circle the letter of the correct negative prefix.

1._____ employed
a. im
b. un
c. dis
d. il

6. _____ responsible
a. un
b. in
c. ir
d. non

2._____ legal
a. il
b. non
c. ir
d. dis

7. _____ agree
a. in
b. im
c. dis
d. il

3._____ polite
a. un
b. non
c. in
d. im

8. _____ appropriate
a. im
b. in
c. non
d. dis

4._____ honest
a. dis
b. un
c. non
d. in

9. _____ violent
a. non
b. dis
c. un
d. in

5._____ successful
a. in
b. ir
c. dis
d. un

10. _____ predictable
a. non
b. im
c. un
d. il

**B.** Circle the letter of the correct word for each commonly confused pair.

1. The movie was _____ long.

   a. quiet          b. quite

2. Many newcomers to the United States _____ to a faster-paced lifestyle.

   a. adapt          b. adopt

3. I try to run a few blocks _____ each day.

   a. farther        b. further

4. Don't _____ drinks down near a computer.

   a. set            b. sit

5. All _____ one boy attended the class.

   a. accept         b. except

6. Gold is more expensive _____ silver.

   a. than           b. then

7. Bread will _____ in the oven as it bakes.

   a. rise           b. raise

8. You can _____ money at a casino.

   a. loose          b. lose

9. A sunny day has a good _____ on my mood.

   a. affect         b. effect

10. A lawyer can _____ you on legal matters.

    a. advice        b. advise

11. The dark clouds made a storm seem _____.

    a. eminent       b. imminent

**C.** Circle the letter of the item that reflects correct form and hyphen usage.

1. The couple ended their _____ marriage in divorce court.

   a. twenty-one-year     b. twenty-one year

2. The college is _____ in the downtown area.

   a. conveniently-located    b. conveniently located

3. The runners were exhausted at the end of the _____ race.

   a. five-mile      b. five-miles

4. _____ cars often use a lot of fuel.

   a. Luxury class   b. Luxury-class

# CHAPTER 7

## A. COMMON PREFIXES

*uni*cycle        *bi*cycle

Prefixes are very productive and very important in the formation of words in the English language. You will see that some words with these prefixes are hyphenated, especially when the prefix ends and the root begins with the same vowel. In some cases, however, there are no rules. In this chapter, hyphens are provided for you when they are needed. You do not need to decide when to add hyphens yourself; you can copy the words with hyphens.

**EXERCISE 1**

Study these prefixes and their meanings.

| PREFIX | MEANING | EXAMPLE |
|--------|---------|---------|
| **pre-** | before | **pre**fix |
| **post-** | after | **post**pone |
| **re-** | again | **re**write |
| **multi-** | many | **multi**colored |
| **bi-** | two | **bi**cycle |

Now, complete each word by adding a prefix from the chart above. Then, write the complete word in the space at the end of the sentence. Each prefix will be used twice.

1. A person who can speak two languages is _____ lingual.

   _____

2. After completing his degree, he continued in _____ graduate studies.

   _____

3. Canned soup is _____ cooked. It does not need to be cooked before eating—only heated.

   _____

4. Someone who feels comfortable living in two cultures is _____ cultural.

   _____

5. The United States is a _____ cultural country in which many different ethnic groups live.

   _____

6. If you don't save your work on your computer, you may lose it and have to _____ do it.

   _____

7. After surgery, most patients remain in the hospital for _____ operative care.

   _____

8. Before kindergarten, many children attend _____ school.

   _____

9. There are many sides to that issue. It's _____ dimensional.

   _____

10. Every now and then, it's a good idea to _____ view the material you have studied.

    _____

**EXERCISE 2**    Study these prefixes and their meanings.

| PREFIX | MEANING | EXAMPLE |
|--------|---------|---------|
| **mis-** | wrong, bad | **mis**understand |
| **anti-** | against, opposing | **anti**war |
| **pro-** | for, supporting | **pro**war |
| **uni-** | one | **uni**cycle |
| **inter-** | between | **inter**national |

Now, complete each word by adding a prefix from the chart. Then, write the complete word in the space at the end of the sentence. Each prefix will be used twice.

1. It's natural to make _____ takes when you're learning a language.

   _____

2. The politician was criticized for favoring large corporations and _____ business policies.

   _____

3. It's not polite to _____ rupt when other people are talking.

   _____

4. The _____ verse encompasses everything, so we cannot imagine its size.

   _____

5. There was an _____ nuclear demonstration at the site of the proposed nuclear power plant.

   _____

6. When traveling in unfamiliar countries, it's easy to _____ interpret people's behavior.

   _____

7. That _____ city bus travels between Las Vegas and Reno, Nevada.

   _____

8. The company wants all of its employees to have the same appearance, so they must wear _____ forms.

   _____

9. Many _____ communist immigrants came to Florida during and after the revolution in Cuba, when the Communists came to power.

   _____

10. People who believe that abortion should not be legal refer to themselves as "_____-life."

    _____

**EXERCISE 3**  Study these prefixes and their meanings.

| PREFIX | MEANING | EXAMPLE |
|--------|---------|---------|
| trans- | across, through | **trans**continental |
| de- | reverse | **de**contaminate |
| *in- | in, inside | **in**put |
| ex- | out, outside | **ex**port |
| over- | too much | **over**eat |

*in- as a negative prefix was introduced in Chapter 6.

Now, complete each word by adding a prefix from the chart. Then, write the complete word in the space at the end of the sentence. Each prefix will be used twice.

1. Before taking off in freezing weather, planes must be _____ iced.

   _____

2. Children can feel hurt when their playmates _____ clude them from their games.

   _____

3. _____ confident drivers sometimes have accidents, because they are too sure of their skills.

   _____

4. The Titanic was on a _____ atlantic crossing when it was sunk by an iceberg.

   _____

5. The college _____ emphasized physical education when closed its sports programs.

   _____

6. Be sure to _____ clude your phone number when you're leaving a telephone message.

   _____

7. The critic said the star's performance in the film was unnatural and described it as "_____ acting."

   _____

8. To buy food from a vending machine, you _____ sert money and push the button to select what you want.

   _____

9. Trucks are often used to _____ port fruit and vegetables across the country.

   _____

10. The student was _____ pelled from the university for stealing and selling exams.

_____

**EXERCISE 4**    Complete the words by adding prefixes from the list. Do not use the same prefix twice.

| pre | post | re | multi | bi |
|-----|------|----|-------|-----|
| mis | anti | pro | uni | inter |
| trans | de | in | ex | over |

1. The family painted the _____ terior of their house gray, and they painted the _____ terior rooms blue and yellow.

2. The population of the United States increased dramatically during the _____-World War II years, when the soldiers returned home and started families.

3. A compass is _____ directional in the sense that it points to only where north is.

4. People who support a woman's decision to end a pregnancy call themselves "_____-choice."

5. Doctors and lawyers may lose their licenses if they are guilty of professional _____ conduct.

6. The doctor prescribed an _____ biotic drug to treat the patient's infection.

7. We can see through a window because the glass in it is _____ parent.

8. You can take the _____ state highway from Chicago, Illinois, to Indianapolis, Indiana.

9. The Central Intelligence Agency employs specialists to _____ code secret messages.

10. We may have _____ conceptions regarding people we have never met. For example, we may expect all Americans to be noisy and rich.

11. The finance committee of the organization prepares a _____ monthly report every sixty days.

12. This knife has a cutting edge, a bottle opener, and other tools. It is _____ purpose.

13. Classrooms in many cities are _____ crowded, because school districts do not have money to hire more teachers or build new schools.

14. I need to _____ organize my files so that I can find all of my documents easily.

**EXERCISE 5**

Write new words by using the words in *italics* and the prefixes in the list. Do not use the same prefix twice.

**over    uni    pre    post    multi**

1. Some states allow families to *pay* their children's college tuition long before the children are old enough to attend. They can _____ college tuition.

2. A country may have a *national* committee to study environmental issues. Sometimes, many countries work together in _____ committees to cooperate in such studies.

3. It's important to *react* appropriately to a situation. If you respond too quickly without thinking, you may _____ and be sorry later.

4. Many articles of clothing are not specific to one *sex* or the other. They are _____ styles.

5. During the *industrial* period, manufacturing was of primary importance. Today, we live in a _____ world where information and services have greater importance.

**EXERCISE 6**    As in Exercise 5, write new words by using the words in *italics* and the prefixes in the list. Do not use the same prefix twice.

**inter    anti    bi    re    mis**

1. *Collegiate* sports are popular. Many students want to participate in them so that they can play against other schools in _____ games.

2. "Don't _____ the wheel" means that we don't need to *invent* things that already exist.

3. We all need to *calculate* our income and expenses to manage our money. If we _____ we may be in trouble.

4. Followers of some religions, such as Quakers, do not believe that *war* is ever justified. These people are always _____.

5. In 1876, the United States celebrated its *centennial*—its one-hundred-year anniversary. In 1976, it celebrated its _____.

# B. EVERYDAY ABBREVIATIONS

Abbreviations are short forms of words used to save time and space in writing. Most abbreviations should not be used in formal or academic writing; however, they are appropriate for use in other situations. The abbreviations in this chapter are all used frequently in daily life.

**EXERCISE 7**    Study these abbreviations related to dates and time. Note which ones use periods and capital letters and which do not.

| ABBREVIATION | MEANING | EXAMPLE |
|---|---|---|
| AD | Latin: *anno domini* (the Christian era) | 1925 AD |
| BC | Before Christ | 3000 BC |
| Jan. | January | Jan. 7 |
| Feb. | February | Feb. 10 |
| Mar. | March | Mar. 22 |
| Apr. | April | Apr. 3 |
| May | Do not abbreviate | May 6 |
| June | Do not abbreviate | June 9 |
| July | Do not abbreviate | July 4 |
| Aug. | August | Aug. 29 |
| Sept. | Sept. | Sept. 14 |
| Oct. | October | Oct. 8 |
| Nov. | November | Nov. 18 |
| Dec. | December | Dec. 15 |
| Sun./Su | Sunday | Sun., Mar. 23 |
| Mon./M | Mon. | Mon., Dec. 2 |
| Tues./Tu | Tues. | Tues., Feb. 22 |
| Wed./W | Wednesday | Wed., May 10 |
| Thurs./Th | Thursday | Thurs., Nov. 30 |
| Fri./F | Friday | Fri., Jan. 12 |
| Sat./Sa | Saturday | Sat., July 17 |
| a.m. | Latin: *ante meridiem* (before noon) | 10:00 a.m. |
| p.m. | Latin: *post meridiem* (after noon) | 10:00 p.m. |

Now, rewrite the sentences using time abbreviations where possible. Also, use numerals for years and times on the clock (3:30, for example).

1. Julius Caesar was assassinated on March 15, forty-four years before Christ.

   _____

   _____

2. Your doctor's appointment is on Monday, January 4, at three o'clock in the afternoon.

   _____

   _____

3. The Greek philosopher Aristotle was born three hundred eighty-four years before Christ and died three hundred twenty-two years before Christ.

   _____

   _____

4. The student club will meet on Tuesday, October 2, from nine o'clock in the morning until eleven o'clock in the morning.

   _____

   _____

5. The Roman Emperor Augustus reigned from twenty-seven years before Christ to year fourteen of the Christian era.

   _____

   _____

6. President John F. Kennedy was born on May 29, 1917. He was shot at twelve-thirty in the afternoon on November 22, 1963, and was pronounced dead at one o'clock in the afternoon that same day.

   _____

   _____

**EXERCISE 8** Without looking at the chart, write the abbreviations for the words. For days of the week, give two forms each. If no abbreviation is possible, write "none." Then, check your answers.

1. Tuesday _____/_____        12. April _____

2. November _____        13. July _____

3. Friday _____/_____        14. Wednesday _____/_____

4. May _____        15. June _____

5. Sunday _____/_____        16. Thursday _____/_____

6. March _____        17. August _____

7. September _____        18. October _____

8. Saturday _____/_____        19. December _____

9. January _____        20. in the morning _____

10. Monday _____/_____        21. in the afternoon _____

11. February _____

**EXERCISE 9** Study these abbreviations related to addresses. Note that all of them use capitals and periods. It is appropriate to use these abbreviations in addressing envelopes but not in running text.

| ABBREVIATION | MEANING | EXAMPLE |
|---|---|---|
| N. | North (NE = Northeast, NW = Northwest) | 211 N. Water |
| S. | South (SE = Southeast, SW = Southwest) | 415 S. Congress |
| E. | East | 619 E. Mulberry |
| W. | West | 874 W. Oakton |
| Apt. | Apartment | Apt. 3B |
| Ave. | Avenue | 500 N. Michigan Ave. |
| Blvd. | Boulevard | 73 Tinley Blvd. |
| Ct. | Court | 85 Hampton Ct. |
| Dr. | Drive | 333 N. Lakeshore Dr. |
| Hwy. | Highway | 44 Founders Hwy. |
| La. | Lane | 99 Melborne La. |
| Pkwy. | Parkway | 300 Diversey Pkwy. |
| Pl. | Place | 43 Warren Pl. |
| Rd. | Road | 88 E. Willow Rd. |
| Rte. | Route | 79 E. Rte 12 |
| Sq. | Square | 10 Washington Sq. |
| St. | Street | 2220 W. Cortez St. |
| Terr. | Terrace | 815 Gordon Terr. |

Now, write names and addresses on the lines using abbreviations and the information given. Follow the model on the envelope below. You may use your own city, state, and zip code, or you may use other cities. Refer to Appendix C for state names, capitals, and postal abbreviations for states.

1. Mary Newman, 33 East Roosevelt Square

   _____

   _____

   _____

Joseph Cranston
766 W. Newmark Pl.,
Apt. 42
Anchorage, AK 99503

2. Mr. Fred Price, 99 South Easton Drive

   _____

   _____

   _____

3. Dr. Herman Brown, 46 North Fifth Street

   _____

   _____

   _____

4. Loretta Olive, 71 West Grant Avenue

   _____

   _____

   _____

5. Gerald Lopez, 100 North Abbot Place

_____

_____

_____

6. Ms. Jane Kowalski, 67 East Butler Court

_____

_____

_____

7. Amanda Rice, 23 South Kinsey Road

_____

_____

_____

8. Ming Chen, 66 Main Street, Northeast

_____

_____

_____

9. Charles O'Connor, 833 Shelton Lane

_____

_____

_____

10. Walsh Insurance, 44 East Grand Boulevard

_____

_____

_____

**EXERCISE 10**    Without looking at the chart, write the abbreviations for the words. Then, check your answers.

1. Avenue _____      8. Lane _____

2. Street _____      9. Apartment _____

3. Highway _____    10. Route _____

4. Boulevard _____  11. Parkway _____

5. Drive _____      12. Square _____

6. Court _____      13. Place _____

7. Terrace _____    14. Road _____

# C. HYPHENS IN WORD DIVISION

Dividing a word in the correct place helps to make your hand·writing easy to read and neat in appearance. In order to div·ide a word appropriately, use the rules you find in this sec·tion.

Although computers will decide how many words will fit on a line when we are typing, we often need to divide words at the ends of lines when we are writing by hand. Hyphens (-) are used for this purpose. For words of two or more syllables, you may consult a dictionary, which will show syllable breaks, usually with a dot (·).

**EXERCISE 11**

Look at the following entries from *The American Heritage English as a Second Language Dictionary*. Where can these words be divided?

1. **por·cu·pine** (**pôr'** kyə pin') *n.* A large rodent covered with long sharp spines that serve as protection.*

2. **re·nowned** (rĭ **nound'**) *adj.* Having renown; famous: *a renowned scientist.*

3. **sup·por·tive** (sə **pôr'** tĭv) *adj.* Providing support, help, or sympathy: *She has been a very supportive friend since my accident.* *

However, not all syllable breaks are the best places to divide words. Use the following rules as a general guide.

*From *The American Heritage English as a Second Language Dictionary*. Copyright © by Houghton Mifflin Company. Reprinted with permission.

# Rules for Dividing Words

Don't divide one-syllable words.

**Examples:**  **walked** and **light** are one-syllable words that cannot be divided.

Don't divide leaving only one letter of a word on a line.

**Examples:**  **a·way** and **i·den·ti·fy** begin with one-letter syllables that should not be left alone. Therefore, **away** cannot be divided. **Identify** can be divided after **iden-.**

Don't divide leaving only two letters of a word on the lower line.

**Example:**  **i·den·ti·fy** has a two-letter final syllable (**fy**) that should not be separated from the rest of the word. **Identify** can be divided only after iden-.

In general, use pronunciation, not spelling, to determine how many syllables a word has.

**Example:**  **explained** has two syllables (**ex·plained**), not three, so it can be divided only between *x* and *p*.

Divide words with prefixes and suffixes between them and their roots. Also, divide compounds between the words that make them.

**Examples:**  **unhappy** is best divided after *un-*, and **watermelon**, a compound, is best divided after *water-*.

Divide between double consonants when appropriate.

**Example:**  **letter** can be divided between the double consonant (**let·ter**), even though both *t*'s are not pronounced.

**EXERCISE 12**

Rewrite the words, using hyphens (-) to show where they can best be divided. If a word cannot be divided, write "no" in the space provided. Use the rules above and a dictionary as needed to help you. Discuss your answers with your classmates, and give reasons for your choices.

1. healthy _____       9. design _____

2. therefore _____     10. equally _____

3. incomplete _____    11. disappearance _____

4. through _____       12. education _____

5. easy _____          13. school _____

6. giving _____        14. university _____

7. attractive _____    15. furthermore _____

8. piano _____         16. blackberry _____

**EXERCISE 13**

As in Exercise 12, rewrite the words, using hyphens (-) to show where they can best be divided. If a word cannot be divided, write "no."

1. calculator _____    9. length _____

2. lifeboat _____      10. electricity _____

3. esophagus _____     11. rope _____

4. tasteless _____     12. busy _____

5. umbrella _____      13. agreement _____

6. climate _____       14. microwave _____

7. practical _____     15. straight _____

8. bilingual _____     16. open _____

***Spelling Word Bank*** In the Spelling Word Bank at the end of this book, write words from this chapter that you find especially difficult or interesting or that are especially good examples.

# CHAPTER 7 TEST

## TOTAL = 25 POINTS, 1 POINT FOR EACH ITEM

**A.** Circle the letter of the choice that is *not* a word.

1. a. miscalculate
   b. mistake
   c. mislingual
2. a. overeat
   b. overatlantic
   c. overcrowded
3. a. exterior
   b. exinterpret
   c. expelled
4. a. intercycle
   b. intercity
   c. interrupt

5. a. reorganize
   b. redo
   c. regraduate
6. a. preschool
   b. prepurpose
   c. prepay
7. a. antiwar
   b. antinuclear
   c. anticonduct
8. a. bicooked
   b. bicentennial
   c. bilingual

9. a. postbiotic
   b. postindustrial
   c. postoperative
10. a. deice
    b. de-emphasize
    c. de-act
11. a. uniform
    b. uniconception
    c. universe
12. a. multiclude
    b. multicultural
    c. multicolored

**B.** Circle the letter of the correct abbreviation.

1. Avenue
   a. Av.
   b. Ave.
2. Tuesday
   a. Tue.
   b. Tues.
3. Street
   a. Str.
   b. St.
4. November
   a. Nov.
   b. Nove.

5. Boulevard
   a. Boul.
   b. Blvd.
6. Wednesday
   a. Wed.
   b. Weds.
7. Thursday
   a. Thur.
   b. Thurs.
8. Apartment
   a. Apt.
   b. Apart.

**C.** Circle the letter of the item that shows the appropriate place or places to divide the word.

1. a. o-ver          b. over
2. a. qual-i-ty      b. qual-ity
3. a. im-pos-si-ble  b. im-poss-i-ble
4. a. dress-ing      b. dres-sing
5. a. tho-ught       b. thought

# CHAPTER 8

## A. COMMON ROOTS

Many roots can be combined with other roots (and also prefixes and suffixes) to form new words. This chapter presents some of the most common roots of Latin and Greek origin.

**EXERCISE 1**   Study these roots and their meanings. Then, answer the questions.

*photographs*

| Root | Meaning |
|------|---------|
| astro | star |
| bio | life |
| cent/centi | hundred/hundredth |
| chron/chrono | time |
| dec/deci | ten/tenth |
| geo | earth |
| graph/graphy | write, draw |
| logy | study |
| meter | measure |
| micro | small |
| phone/phono | sound |
| photo | light |
| psych/psycho | mind |
| tech/techno | skill or science |
| tele | distant |
| therm/thermo | heat |

1. In these roots, the letters *ch* are pronounced like *k*. Which three roots are spelled with these letters?

   _____, _____, _____

2. The letters *ph* are pronounced like *f*. Which three roots are spelled with these letters?

   _____, _____, _____

3. The letters *ps* are pronounced like *s*. Which root is spelled with these letters?

   _____

**EXERCISE 2**

Combine roots from the chart in Exercise 1 to make words with the given definitions.

1. study of the earth: _____

2. distant sound: _____

3. measure of one hundredth: _____

4. write with light: _____

5. measurer of heat: _____

6. study of the mind: _____

7. measure of one tenth: _____

8. small sound: _____

9. study of life: _____

10. study of time: _____

11. study of a skill: _____

12. distant writing: _____

13. writing about someone's life: _____

14. drawing of the earth: _____

15. study of the stars: _____

**EXERCISE 3**    Complete the words with roots from the chart in Exercise 1. Then, write the complete words in the spaces at the ends of the sentences. The words in *italics* will help you choose the appropriate roots.

1. A camera that can take pictures of things *far* away has a _____ photo lens.

_____

2. A device that *measures* barometric (air) pressure is a baro_____.

_____

3. A doctor of the *mind* is a _____iatrist.

_____

4. A scientist uses a _____scope to see very *small* things.

_____

5. We watch *distant* signals on a _____vision.

_____

6. In a car, the speedo_____ *measures* how fast we're driving.

_____

7. We need _____communications equipment to contact people who *aren't near* us.

_____

8. The *light* coming from the _____copy machine tells us it's working.

_____

9. When we *write* compositions, we organize them by forming para_____s.

_____

10. A period of *ten* years is a _____ade.

_____

11. A _____pede is an animal with *one hundred* feet.

_____

12. A person who applies *science* in his or her job is a _____nician.

_____

13. A person who travels in *outer space* is an _____naut.

_____

14. A *measure* across a circle is the dia_____.

_____

15. One treatment for illnesses of the *mind* is _____therapy.

_____

16. The study of *stars*, planets, and other features of the universe is

_____nomy.

_____

17. A _____ic illness is one that lasts for a long *time*.

_____

18. Fabric that conserves *heat* is used to make _____al underwear.

_____

19. _____logical order is used to tell about things in the order in which

they happened in *time*.

_____

20. A supervisor who feels he or she must know about and be involved in every *small*

decision is called a _____manager.

_____

**EXERCISE 4**  Study these roots and their meanings.

*eruption*

| Root | Meaning |
|------|---------|
| aero | air |
| cide | kill |
| dict | say, tell |
| form | shape |
| milli | thousand/thousandth |
| mit | send |
| port | carry |
| reg | rule |
| rupt | break |
| scribe | write |

Now, complete the words by adding roots from the chart. Then, write the complete words in the spaces at the ends of the sentences. The words in *italics* will help you choose the appropriate roots.

1. A person who *kills* himself or herself commits sui_____.

   _____

2. A device that *sends* a signal is a trans_____ter.

   _____

3. A leader who *tells* a country what to do is a _____ator.

   _____

4. A spelling pattern that follows a *rule* is _____ular.

   _____

5. A business that *carries* things to other countries for sale is an ex_____ business.

   _____

6. A business that *carries* things from other countries back to a country for sale is an im_____ business.

   _____

7. Things that have the same *shape* are uni_____.

   _____

8. TV weather reporters try to pre_____ what type of weather we will have. They *tell* us what they think will happen.

   _____

9. The *killing* of a human being is a homi_____.

   _____

10. The jeweler in_____d the couple's names in their wedding rings. He *wrote* their names on the gold bands.

    _____

11. A _____liter is one *thousandth* of a liter. It's a small amount.

    _____

12. The _____space industry produces vehicles that travel through the *air* beyond our planet.

    _____

13. The government makes *rules* or laws to _____ulate business and industry.

    _____

14. Vegetables and fruit are *carried* across the country. Trucks are often used to trans_____ the food.

    _____

15. A volcano can lie quietly for many years without any lava *breaking* through its surface. Then, it can suddenly e_____.

_____

16. When we tell about something in *writing*, we de_____ it.

_____

17. It's not polite to *break* into a conversation between two people. When you do this, you inter_____ them.

_____

18. When you sub_____ something, you *send* it where it should go.

_____

19. A _____meter is one *thousandth* of a meter.

_____

20. When we have in_____ ation, our ideas take *shape*.

_____

# B. SPELLING OF WORDS FOR COMMON SYMBOLS

Symbols are very useful to quickly and easily substitute for words in informal notes and messages. In formal and academic writing, however, it is best to spell out the words rather than use symbols. Most numbers are also spelled out in formal writing.

Study the symbols and corresponding words in the chart. Note that three of the symbols have more than one meaning.

| Symbol | Word | Symbol | Word |
| --- | --- | --- | --- |
| @ | at | % | percent |
| $ | dollar(s) | & | and |
| ¢ | cent(s) | + | plus(es) |
| # | pound (s) | – | minus(es) |
| # | number | – | from . . . to |
| × | times | = | equals |
| ÷ | divided by | ≈ | approximately |
| / | per | $^c/_o$ | in care of |
| / | for | < | less than |
| / | or | > | more than |

_[handwritten in top margin: Can]_ _[handwritten in top margin: turn]_

**EXERCISE 5** | Rewrite the sentences, changing the symbols to words. Also, change the numbers to words.

1. You can send the package to me $^C/_O$ my employer @ our downtown office.

_You can send the package to me in care of my employer at our downtown_

2. Please complete item #2 before you do #3.

_Please complete item from before number_ _[handwritten above: number]_

3. 2 + 2 = 4.

_four plus tow equals four_

4. He pays >50% of his income in taxes.

_He pays more than 50 percent of his income_

5. Take this medicine 4✕/day.

_Take this medicine four times per day_

6. The First City Bank loan rate was 1% < the rate at Community Bank.

_The first city Bank loan rate was less than 1 Percent_

7. The project will cost ≈ $20,000.

_The project will cost approximately_

8. We bought 12 muffins @ 2/$1 and 5# of coffee.

_____

9. Doctors say it's best to get >7 hours of sleep/night.

_Doctors say it's best to get more 7 hours of sleep per night_

10. 8 − 2 = 6.

_eight minus_

11. We expect the meeting to last 2–3 hours.

_we expect the meeting to last from 2 to 3 ho_

12. Gasoline prices can vary as much as 50¢/gallon between the city and suburbs.

_Gasoline prices can vary as much as 50 cent per_

_[handwritten at bottom: I am chixing]_

**EXERCISE 6**

As in Exercise 5, rewrite the sentences, changing the symbols and numbers to words.

1. It's good to consider all the +s and −s when making a decision.

_____

2. A good microscope can magnify images 1,000× or more.

_____

3. Please call me @10:00 or earlier.

_____

4. The telephone company has raised its call rates by 10¢/minute.

_____

5. If a student has a job, it can affect his/her performance in class.

_____

6. 20 ÷ 4 = 5.

_____

7. The doctor will be seeing patients 9:00−4:00.

_____

8. Write your phone # & address on the application.

_____

9. You may contact me by e-mail/telephone @ my office.

_____

10. There were ≈3,000 students and >5,000 guests at the graduation ceremony.

_____

11. Student jobs start @ $10/hour.

_____

12. The recommended dosage for that medicine is 1 tablet/50# of body weight.

_____

# C. SOUND-SPELLING CORRESPONDENCE WITH VOWELS

It's important to be able to spell words that you hear but haven't seen in print or don't remember how to spell. In English, the vowel sounds have the most variation, so that is where most problems arise. Knowing the common spelling patterns for vowel sounds will make it easier for you to predict and recognize the spelling of words you know from listening and speaking. You may refer to the inside front cover of this book for a summary of the vowel sounds and symbols.

**EXERCISE 7**    Study these spelling variations for the /ā/ sound.

| | |
|---|---|
| **ā  Common spellings:** | *a*, as in *April* |
| | *a (consonant) silent* |
| | *e*, as in *same* |
| | *ai*, as in *wait* |
| | *ay*, as in *play* |
| | *ei*, as in *eight* |
| **Less common spellings:** | *ea*, as in *reak* |
| | *ey*, as in *they* |

Now, complete each word with one of the possible spellings for the /ā/ sound.

1. not early:          l _____ t _____

2. opposite of *night*:    d _____ _____

3. kitchen furniture:     t _____ bl _____

4. person next door:     n _____ _____ ghbor

5. wonderful:         gr _____ _____ t

6. country in Europe:    Sp _____ _____ n

7. homonym of *wait*:    w _____ _____ ght

8. blood carrier:        v _____ _____ n

9. *John* or *Mary*:     n _____ m _____

10. after April:         M _____ _____

11. dried grape:        r _____ _____ sin

12. what you write on:    p _____ per

13. attention getter:     h _____ _____

14. opposite of *love*:    h _____ t _____

**EXERCISE 8**  Study this common spelling for the /ă/ sound.

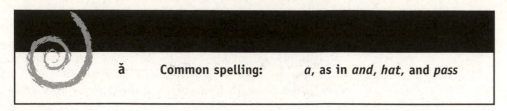

ă    **Common spelling:**    *a*, as in *and*, *hat*, and *pass*

Now, circle the letters that represent the / ă / sound in the words.

1. S a t u r d a y        7. A t l a n t a

2. h a v e                8. b a n a n a

3. l a s t                9. m a t h e m a t i c s

4. b a n d               10. c a l c u l a t o r

5. A f r i c a           11. s a l a d

6. a c t o r             12. g a s o l i n e

**EXERCISE 9**  Study these spelling variations for the /ē/ sound.

ē   **Common spellings:**    *e*, as in *he*

*ee*, as in *sleep*

*ea*, as in *team*

*e (consonant)silent e*, as in *these*

*ey*, as in *key*

*ie*, as in *believe*

*y*, as in *busy*

**Less common spelling:**    *ei*, as in *either*

*i*, as in *police*

Now, complete each word with one of the possible spellings of the /ē/ sound.

1. polite word:        pl_____ _____ se

2. brother's daughter:  n _____ _____ ce

3. avenue:             str _____ _____ t

4. electronic thing:    mach _____ ne

5. green vegetable:     p _____ _____

6. whole:               compl _____ t _____

7. $$$:                 mon _____ _____

8. part of a cake:      p _____ _____ ce

9. fuel for a car:      gasol_____ _____ne

10. same:               _____ qual

11. opposite of give:   rec_____ _____ve

12. robber:             th _____ _____ f

13. watched:            s _____ _____ n

14. horse relative:     donk _____ _____

15. fast:               quickl _____

16. write again:        r _____ write

**EXERCISE 10**    Study these spelling variations for the /ĕ/ sound.

| ĕ | **Common spellings:** | *e*, as in *egg* |
| | | *ea*, as in *head* |
| | **Less common spellings:** | *a*, as in *many* |
| | | *ue*, as in *guess* |

Now, circle the letters that represent the /ĕ/ sound in the words.

1. b r e a k f a s t        5. s e n d          9. a n y

2. b e t t e r              6. g u e s t        10. b r e a d

3. e l e m e n t            7. p r e s i d e n t    11. h e a l t h y

4. r e a d y                8. t w e n t y      12. S e p t e m b e r

**EXERCISE 11**    Study these spelling variations for the /ī/ sound.

| ī | **Common spellings:** | *i*, as in *idea* |
| | | *i* (consonant) *silent e*, as in *nice* |
| | | *ie*, as in *tie* |
| | | *y*, as in *my* |
| | **Less common spellings:** | *uy*, as in *buy* |
| | | *ye*, as in *dye* |

Now, complete each word by adding one of the spelling variations for the /ī/ sound.

1. opposite of *day*:        n _____ ght

2. ask for a job:            appl _____

3. dessert:                  p _____ _____

4. fashion:                  st _____ le

5. question word:           wh _____

6. thing:                    _____ tem

7. type:                     k _____ nd

8. not the truth:           l _____ _____

9. not public:               pr _____ vate

10. opposite of *lose*:      f _____ nd

11. not rude:                pol _____ t _____

12. male person:             g _____ _____

13. 5:                       f _____ v _____

14. opposite of *hello*:     good-b_____ _____

---

**EXERCISE 12**   Study these spelling variations for the /ĭ/ sound.

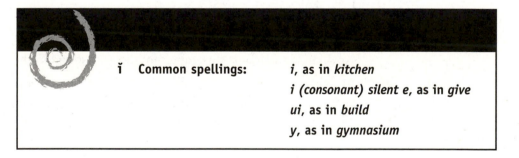

| ĭ | Common spellings: | i, as in *kitchen* |
|---|---|---|
| | | i (consonant) silent e, as in *give* |
| | | ui, as in *build* |
| | | y, as in *gymnasium* |

Now, complete each word by adding one of the spelling variations for the /ĭ/ sound.

1. present:                  g _____ ft

2. 1/60 hour:                m _____ nute

3. opposite of *die*:        l _____ v _____

4. cold season:              w _____ nter

5. instrument:               g _____ _____ tar

6. organization:             s _____ stem

7. Nile:                     r _____ ver

8. one of ten:               f _____ nger

9. study of ideas:          ph _____ losophy

10. # or %:                 s _____ mbol

11. not innocent:           g _____ _____ lty

12. family member:          relat _____ v _____

13. from that time:         s _____ nce

14. tempo:                  rh _____ thm

**EXERCISE 13**    Study these spelling variations for the /ŏ/ sound.

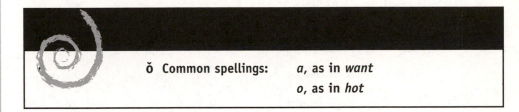

ŏ **Common spellings:**    *a*, as in *want*

                          *o*, as in *hot*

Now, circle the letters that represent the /ŏ/ sound in each word.

1. w a n t              7. a d o p t

2. p a r k              8. w a t c h

3. p o l i t i c s      9. s h o c k

4. d o c t o r          10. p o p u l a r

5. s t o p p e d        11. g a r a g e

6. C o l o r a d o      12. h o n e s t

**EXERCISE 14**    Write the vowel sound that is represented by the letters in italics. Choose from /ā/, /ă/, /ē/, /ĕ/, /ī/, /ĭ/, and /ŏ/. Refer to earlier exercises in this section, as needed.

1. inst*ea*d _____          9. sc*e*ne _____

2. *i*con _____             10. sh*i*p _____

3. pl*ai*n _____            11. c*a*bin _____

4. m*i*nd _____             12. fl*a*me _____

5. sh*o*p _____             13. ic*o*n _____

6. m*ea*n _____             14. h*a*ppen _____

7. m*ea*nt _____            15. subl*i*me _____

8. f*i*t _____

***Spelling Word Bank***    In the Spelling Word Bank at the end of this book, write words from this chapter that you find especially difficult or interesting or that are especially good examples.

# CHAPTER 8 TEST

## TOTAL = 25 POINTS, 1 POINT FOR EACH ITEM

**A.** Circle the letter of the item that is correctly spelled.

1. a. cronological     b. chronological     c. kronological

2. a. sychiatrist     b. phychiatrist     c. psychiatrist

3. a. milimeter     b. millimeter     c. milimeeter

4. a. airospace     b. aerospace     c. earospace

5. a. thermometer     b. therometer     c. termometer

6. a. astranaut     b. asternaut     c. astronaut

7. a. homicide     b. homiside     c. homocide

8. a. biography     b. biografy     c. biogrophy

9. a. gealogy     b. geolagy     c. geology

10. a. transmiter     b. transmeter     c. transmitter

**B.** Write the word or words for each symbol in the space provided.

1. % _____

2. ¢ _____

3. ≈ _____

4. < _____

5. % _____

**Online Teaching Center**

**C.** Listen to the vowel sounds as your instructor pronounces each word. Then, circle the letter of the item that spells that word. You will hear each word twice.

1. a. lame    b. lime        6. a. pie    b. pea

2. a. fine    b. fin        7. a. beet    b. bet

3. a. wheel    b. while        8. a. relieve    b. relive

4. a. meddle    b. middle        9. a. band    b. bond

5. a. black    b. block        10. a. slip    b. slap

# CHAPTER 9

## A. COMMONLY MISSPELLED WORDS

*cemetery*

Many of the most commonly misspelled words in the English language for academic purposes were introduced earlier in this book. Here are some others for which, unfortunately, there are no simple rules. Try to remember them according to the patterns presented in this section or according to some memory aid of your own. For example, English has many words that end in −*ary* (*boundary, contrary, January, revolutionary,* etc.) but very few that end in −*ery. Stationery* (writing paper) and *cemetery* (burial place for the dead) are two of those few −*ery* words. You might remember that a *cemetery* is not a place where you would want to spend a lot of time; therefore, you would almost never use −*ery*.

**EXERCISE 1**   Study these commonly misspelled nouns that end in −*ance* and −*ence*. Note that the pronunciation of −*ance* and −*ence* is identical.

| | | | |
|---|---|---|---|
| absence | convenience | intelligence | precedence |
| abundance | correspondence | interference | preference |
| acquaintance | dependence | maintenance | reference |
| appearance | difference | obedience | relevance |
| assistance | dominance | occurrence | sentence |
| attendance | existence | performance | violence |
| coincidence | experience | permanence | |
| conscience | insurance | perseverance | |

*Note: A number of these words have corresponding* −ant *and* −ent *forms, such as* abundant, convenient, intelligent, relevant, *and* violent. *The vowels for the* −nt *and* −nce *forms are the same.*

Now, write each word in the list under the appropriate heading in the table. Which group is larger?

| −*ance* | | −*ence* | |
|---|---|---|---|
| | | | |
| | | | |
| | | | |
| | | | |
| | | | |
| | | | |
| | | | |
| | | | |
| | | | |
| | | | |
| | | | |

**EXERCISE 2**

Study these frequently misspelled words that have one or more pairs of double letters.

| | | | |
|---|---|---|---|
| accidentally | disappoint | necessary | recommend |
| accommodate | embarrass | occasionally | roommate |
| accumulate | exaggerate | opponent | succeed |
| across | fulfill | opportunity | sufficient |
| address | guarantee | possession | tomorrow |
| annual | immediately | possibility | usually |
| appreciate | millionaire | practically | |
| committee | misspelled | really | |

Now, write the words in the list under the appropriate headings in the table.

| *One double letter* | | *Two or more double letters* | |
|---|---|---|---|
| | | | |
| | | | |
| | | | |
| | | | |
| | | | |
| | | | |
| | | | |
| | | | |
| | | | |
| | | | |

**EXERCISE 3**   Study these words that all contain *ei* or *ie*.

| | | | |
|---|---|---|---|
| achieve | deceive | leisure | relieve |
| believe | either | neighbor | seize |
| caffeine | foreign | neither | thief |
| ceiling | forfeit | perceive | weight |
| chief | grieve | protein | weird |
| conceive | height | receive | yield |

Now, write each word under the appropriate heading in the table.

| ei | | ie | |
|---|---|---|---|
| | | | |
| | | | |
| | | | |
| | | | |
| | | | |
| | | | |
| | | | |
| | | | |
| | | | |

**EXERCISE 4**   Complete the words from Exercises 1, 2, and 3 by filling in the missing letters. Try not to look at the lists until you've finished.

1. relev _____ nce

2. conc_____ _____ ve

3. com _____ it _____ e _____

4. abs _____ nce

5. mi _____ _____ pell

6. nec_____ s _____ ary

7. c _____ _____ ling

8. w _____ _____ rd

9. pos _____ es _____ ion

10. insur _____ nce

11. tom _____ r _____ ow

12. recom _____ end

13. su _____ _____ _____ ed

14. depend _____ nce

15. embar _____ a _____ _____

16. bel _____ _____ ve

17. ch _____ _____ f

18. attend _____ nce

19. o _____ ponent

20. sent _____ nce

**EXERCISE 5**    As in Exercise 4, complete the words by filling in the missing letters.

1. ro _____ m _____ ate

2. s _____ _____ ze

3. n _____ _____ ghbor

4. mi _____ _____ ionaire

5. rel _____ _____ ve

6. viol _____ nce

7. y _____ _____ ld

8. persever _____ nce

9. mainten _____ nce

10. op _____ ortunity

11. h _____ _____ ght

12. intellig _____ nce

13. conveni _____ nce

14. a _____ _____ ress

15. exag _____ erate

16. a _____ nual

17. appear _____ nce

18. rec _____ _____ ve

19. experi _____ nce

20. ac _____ o _____ s

**EXERCISE 6**    As in the preceding exercises, complete the words with the missing letters.

1. differ _____ nce

2. ac _____ identa _____ _____ y

3. occur _____ _____ nce

4. ac _____ umulate

5. perc _____ _____ ve

6. domin _____ nce

7. for _____ _____ gn

8. oc _____ as _____ onal _____ y

9. _____ _____ ther

10. refer _____ nce

11. fulfi _____ _____

12. assist _____ nce

13. prefer _____ nce

14. i _____ mediat _____ _____ y

15. exist _____ nce

16. ach _____ _____ ve

17. n _____ _____ ther

18. coincid _____ nce

19. a _____ com _____ odate

20. abund _____ nce

## B. BRITISH VERSUS AMERICAN SPELLING

British spelling of the English language is used in many parts of Europe and Asia, as well as Canada. American spelling is used in the United States and often in Central and South America. The variety you use should reflect where you are and who your readers are. Most words are spelled identically in British and American English. However, there are a few patterns that differ. Fortunately, the most common spelling differences are regular, like the following examples.

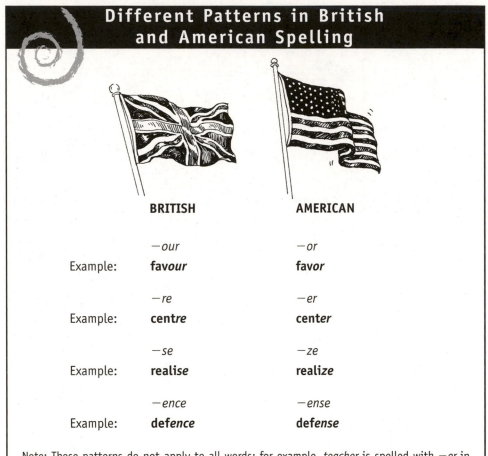

### Different Patterns in British and American Spelling

|  | BRITISH | AMERICAN |
|---|---|---|
|  | —our | —or |
| Example: | **favour** | **favor** |
|  | —re | —er |
| Example: | **centre** | **center** |
|  | —se | —ze |
| Example: | **realise** | **realize** |
|  | —ence | —ense |
| Example: | **defence** | **defense** |

Note: These patterns do not apply to all words; for example, *teacher* is spelled with —er in both British and American English, and *exercise* is spelled with —ise in both.

**EXERCISE 7** | Rewrite the British words using American spelling. Follow the patterns given above.

1. neighbour  _____

2. analyse  _____

3. licence  _____

4. labour  _____

5. metre  _____

6. offence  _____

7. humour  _____

8. paralyse  _____

9. colour  _____

10. theatre        _____

11. honour         _____

12. fibre          _____

13. favourite      _____

14. organise       _____

15. litre          _____

16. memorise       _____

17. realise        _____

18. behaviour      _____

19. centre         _____

20. defence        _____

21. recognise      _____

22. flavour        _____

23. harbour        _____

24. economise      _____

25. tumour         _____

**EXERCISE 8**

In each of the following sentences, there is *one* word with British spelling. Find the word, and write the American spelling above it. Use a dictionary, as necessary.

*Note: These words do not follow the patterns of the words in the preceding exercise.*

1. The man was sentenced to ten years in gaol for the crime.

2. Charles Lindbergh flew an aeroplane from North America to Europe.

3. You can have a watch repaired at a jewellery store.

4. Learning a language involves a lot of practise.

5. The radio programme quickly became popular.

6. Stores accept credit cards and cheques for payment.

7. Researchers found a connexion between smoking and cancer.

8. Pyjamas are popular sleepwear for both men and women.

9. Instructors often ask students to write more than one draught of a composition.

10. I learnt quite a bit of Spanish during my summer in Mexico.

11. We were late to work because our car had a flat tyre.

12. An encyclopaedia contains articles on many different subjects.

# C. MORE SOUND-SPELLING CORRESPONDENCE WITH VOWELS

This is a continuation of vowels sounds, adding to what was presented in Chapter 8. Remember that you can see an overview of the symbols on the inside front cover of this book.

**EXERCISE 9**    Study these spelling variations for the /ō/ sound.

> **ō Common spellings:**    *o,* as in *no*
> *oa,* as in *road*
> *o (consonant) silent e,* as in *home*
> *oe,* as in *toe*
> *ou,* as in *although*
> *ow,* as in *know*

Now, complete each word by adding one of the possible spellings for the /ō/ sound.

1. opposite of *under*:      _____ ver

2. small ship:      b _____ _____ t

3. opposite of *stay*:      g _____

4. get larger:      gr _____ _____

5. past of *speak*:      sp _____ k _____

6. capital of Japan:      T _____ ky _____

7. not quite all:      m _____ st

8. not fast:      sl _____ _____

9. leaves:      g _____ _____ s

10. body part:      sh _____ _____ lder

11. past of *write*:      wr _____ t _____

12. cleaner:      s _____ _____ p

13. less than a minute:      m _____ ment

14. spirit:      s _____ _____ l

**EXERCISE 10**   Study these spelling variations for the /ô/ sound.

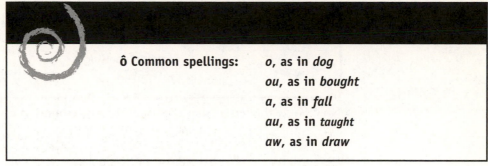

ô Common spellings:   *o*, as in *dog*
                       *ou*, as in *bought*
                       *a*, as in *fall*
                       *au*, as in *taught*
                       *aw*, as in *draw*

Now, complete each word by adding one of the possible spellings for the /ô/ sound.

1. opposite of *on*:      _____ ff

2. past of *catch*:       c _____ _____ ght

3. supervisor:            b _____ ss

4. summer month:         _____ _____ gust

5. past of see:           s _____ _____

6. popular drink:         c _____ ffee

7. American city:         B _____ ston

8. not short:             l _____ ng

9. past of think:         th _____ _____ ght

10. pepper's partner:     s _____ lt

11. speak:                t _____ lk

12. melody:               s _____ ng

13. terrible:             _____ _____ ful

14. reason:               c _____ _____ se

**EXERCISE 11**   Study these spelling variations for the /ou/ sound.

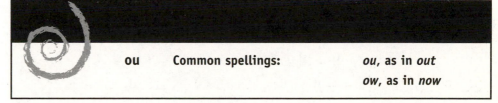

ou   Common spellings:   *ou*, as in *out*
                         *ow*, as in *now*

Now, circle the letters that represent the /ou/ sound in each word.

1. m o u n t a i n        7. n o u n

2. c o w                  8. p o u n d

3. f l o w e r            9. p o w e r

4. v o w e l             10. s h o u t

5. t h o u s a n d       11. d o w n t o w n

6. p r o n o u n c e     12. f o u n d a t i o n

**EXERCISE 12**    Study these spelling variations for the /oi/ sound.

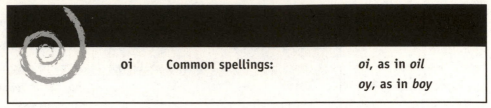

| | oi | Common spellings: | *oi*, as in *oil* |
| | | | *oy*, as in *boy* |

Now, circle the letters that represent the /oi/ sound in each word.

1. n o i s e
2. p o i n t
3. p o i s o n o u s
4. v o i c e
5. d e s t r o y
6. o y s t e r

7. c h o i c e
8. D e t r o i t
9. e m p l o y m e n t
10. a n n o y a n c e
11. u n a v o i d a b l e
12. j o y o u s

**EXERCISE 13**    Study these spelling variations for the /ōō/ sound.

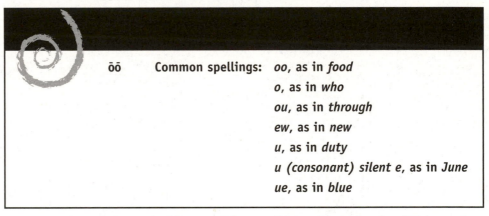

| | ōō | Common spellings: | *oo*, as in *food* |
| | | | *o*, as in *who* |
| | | | *ou*, as in *through* |
| | | | *ew*, as in *new* |
| | | | *u*, as in *duty* |
| | | | *u (consonant) silent e*, as in *June* |
| | | | *ue*, as in *blue* |

Now, complete each word with one of the possible spellings for the /ōō/ sound.

1. change places:        m _____ ve
2. street:               aven _____ _____
3. day of the week:      T _____ _____ sday
4. college:              sch _____ _____ l
5. past of *throw*:      thr _____ _____
6. not a lie:            tr _____ th
7. not polite:           r _____ d _____
8. several people:       gr _____ _____ p
9. opposite of *win*:    l _____ se
10. Missouri city: St.   L _____ _____ is
11. follow:              purs _____ _____
12. singular of *teeth*: t _____ _____ th
13. liquid meal:         s _____ _____ p
14. select:              ch _____ _____ se

**EXERCISE 14**    Study these spelling variations for the /ŏŏ/ sound.

| /ŏŏ/ | Common spellings: | oo, as in *cook* |
|------|-------------------|------------------|
|      |                   | ou, as in *would* |
|      |                   | u, as in *put* |

Now, complete each word by adding one of the possible spellings for the /ŏŏ/ sound.

1. past of *can:*              c _____ _____ ld

2. something to read:          b _____ _____ k

3. ought to:                   sh _____ _____ ld

4. sweet ingredient:           s _____ gar

5. opposite of *pull*:         p _____ sh

6. past of stand:              st _____ _____ d

7. part of NYC:                Br _____ _____ klyn

8. not bad:                    g _____ _____ d

9. small tree:                 b _____ sh

10. sweet snack:               c _____ _____ kie

11. furniture material:        w _____ _____ d

12. past of *take:*            t _____ _____ k

**EXERCISE 15**    Study these spelling variations for the /ŭ/ sound.

> ŭ    **Common spellings:**    *u*, as in *but*
>                              *o(consonant) silent e*, as in *some*
>                              *o*, as in *London*
>                              *ou*, as in *tough*

Now, complete each word by adding one of the possible spellings for the /ŭ/ sound.

1.  fortunate:              l _____ cky

2.  arrive:                 c _____ me

3.  opposite of *hate:*     l _____ ve

4.  problems:               tr _____ _____ ble

5.  male child:             s _____ n

6.  opposite of *over:*     _____ nder

7.  female parent:          m _____ ther

8.  sweet ingredient:       h _____ ney

9.  aunt's son:             c _____ _____ sin

10. thirty days:            m _____ nth

11. yellow condiment:       m _____ stard

12. baker:                  _____ ven

13. seventh day:            S _____ nday

14. nation:                 c _____ _____ ntry

**EXERCISE 16**    Write the vowel sound that is represented by the letters in italics. Choose from /ō/, /ô/, /ou/, /oi/, /o͞o/, /o͝o/ and /ŭ/. Refer to earlier exercises in this section, as needed.

1. *o*ften          _____

2. j*u*dge          _____

3. br*ou*ght        _____

4. c*oo*l           _____

5. Illin*oi*s       _____

6. r*ou*gh          _____

7. h*ou*se          _____

8. *ow*n            _____

9. t*u*ne           _____

10. ph*o*ne         _____

11. sh*oo*k         _____

12. sh*ow*er        _____

13. s*oy*bean       _____

14. potat*oe*s      _____

15. f*oo*t          _____

***Spelling Word Bank***    In the Spelling Word Bank at the end of this book, write words from this chapter that you find especially difficult or interesting or that are especially good examples.

# CHAPTER 9 TEST

## TOTAL = 25 POINTS, 1 POINT FOR EACH ITEM

**A.** Circle the letter of the correctly spelled word.

1. a. interference      b. interferance
2. a. wieght            b. weight
3. a. dissapoint        b. disappoint
4. a. beleive           b. believe
5. a. acquaintance      b. acquaintence
6. a. leisure           b. liesure
7. a. preferance        b. preference
8. a. embarrass         b. embarass
9. a. neccesary         b. necessary
10. a. yeild            b. yield

**B.** Write the American equivalents of these British spellings.

1. favourite    _____
2. programme  _____
3. licence      _____
4. centre       _____
5. organise     _____

**C.** Listen to the vowel sounds as your instructor pronounces each word. Then, circle the letter of the item that spells that word. You will hear each word twice.

1. a. bow      b. boy
2. a. could    b. cooed
3. a. pound    b. pond
4. a. but      b. boot
5. a. shout    b. shut
6. a. grow     b. grew
7. a. wool     b. wall
8. a. noise    b. nose
9. a. saw      b. sue
10. a. toes    b. toys

# REVIEW OF CHAPTERS 6 – 9

**EXERCISE 1**

Fill in the blanks by adding the negative prefixes from Chapter 6 below to the words in *italics*.

unil     im     ir     in     non     dis

1. Lying and stealing are not *moral*. They are _____.

2. Children are *dependent* on their parents. Often they become

   _____ when they graduate from college.

3. Eating while driving is *legal*. Drinking alcohol while driving is

   _____.

4. When we buy something new, we expect it to be in *perfect* condition. We may

   return it to the store if it is _____.

5. If 95 percent of your answers are *correct,* then 5 percent of them are

   _____.

6. *Walk* and *paint* are *regular* verbs. *Run* and *draw* are _____.

7. Water is *necessary* to sustain life. Chocolate cake is wonderful but _____.

8. The decisions of some lower courts are *reversible* by higher courts. Decisions by

   the Supreme Court, however, are _____.

9. Corn is the most popular vegetable in the United States. Therefore, many

   people must *like* it. Relatively few people _____ corn.

10. Our first efforts are often _____; however, if we continue

    to try, we usually become *successful*.

11. When you have a job, you are *responsible* for arriving on time and completing your

    work. Being late and not finishing work are _____.

12. If the signature of a famous artist on a painting is *legible,* its value is increased.

    If the signature is _____, however, the value is reduced.

13. It some cultures, it is *polite* to repeatedly offer more food to a guest who refuses

    it. In other cultures, it's _____.

14. The union leader said that the pay raise was a *negotiable* issue, but that better

    pension and health care plans were _____.

15. Fruit that is not yet ripe is _____. Fruit that is ripe is

    *mature.*

**EXERCISE 2** Combine prefixes with roots to form words that you studied in Chapter 8. Use each prefix and root only once. Write the words in the spaces provided.

**Prefixes:**                       **Roots:**

| | | | |
|---|---|---|---|
| 1. pre- | 9. uni- | national | industrial |
| 2. post- | 10. inter- | form | put |
| 3. re- | 11. trans- | emphasize | pel |
| 4. multi- | 12. de- | choice | war |
| 5. bi- | 13. in- | parent | pay |
| 6. mis- | 14. ex- | colored | invent |
| 7. anti- | 15. over- | react | |
| 8. pro- | | centennial | understand |

1. _____     9. _____

2. _____     10. _____

3. _____     11. _____

4. _____     12. _____

5. _____     13. _____

6. _____     14. _____

7. _____     15. _____

8. _____

**EXERCISE 3** Write a root that you studied in Chapter 8 for each definition. Then, write one or more words with that root in the space provided.

*telephone*

                  **Root**                         **Word(s)**

1. star:     _____     _____

                                                  _____

2. kill:     _____     _____

                                                  _____

3. light:     _____     _____

                                                  _____

4. skill: _____   _____
_____

5. break: _____   _____
_____

6. distant: _____   _____
_____

7. air: _____   _____
_____

8. study of: _____   _____
_____

9. write: _____   _____
_____

10. mind: _____   _____
_____

11. ten: _____   _____
_____

12. time: _____   _____
_____

13. heat: _____   _____
_____

14. carry: _____   _____
_____

**EXERCISE 4**   As in Exercise 3, write a root that you studied in Chapter 8 for each definition. Then, write one or more words with that root in the space provided.

| | **Root** | **Word(s)** |
|---|---|---|

1. measure: _____   _____
_____

2. life: _____   _____
_____

3. rule: _____   _____
_____

4. thousand: _____   _____
_____

5. earth: _____   _____
_____

6. say, tell: _____   _____
_____

7. write, draw: _____    _____

                                     _____

8. sound: _____          _____

                                     _____

9. shape: _____          _____

                                     _____

10. send: _____          _____

                                     _____

11. small: _____         _____

                                     _____

12. hundred: _____       _____

                                     _____

**EXERCISE 5**   Based on the spelling of the *italicized* vowel sounds, circle the letter of the item that has a different vowel sound from the other words in the group. You studied these sounds in Chapters 8 and 9.

1. a. b*ea*m
   b. n*ee*d
   c. r*e*d

2. a. g*oe*s
   b. c*oi*n
   c. l*oa*d

3. a. t*a*ke
   b. r*ai*d
   c. b*a*d

4. a. sl*e*pt
   b. c*a*n
   c. h*ea*d

5. a. h*o*ne
   b. m*ow*
   c. t*oo*l

6. a. p*u*t
   b. c*au*ght
   c. t*a*ll

7. a. b*u*t
   b. c*ou*ld
   c. b*oo*k

8. a. h*u*m
   b. m*o*nth
   c. b*oi*l

9. a. sk*y*
   b. p*i*le
   c. p*i*n

10. a. p*oi*nt
    b. p*ow*er
    c. pr*ou*d

11. a. c*oo*l
    b. d*o*ne
    c. p*u*ff

12. a. m*i*st
    b. g*ui*ld
    c. s*i*te

13. a. f*oo*l
    b. thr*ow*
    c. fl*ew*

14. a. c*oa*l
    b. p*o*t
    c. w*a*tch

**EXERCISE 6**  Write the missing member of each commonly confused pair of words which you studied in Chapter 6.

*costume*

1. special clothes: *costume*    way of behaving: _____

2. comparison word: *than*    at that time: _____

3. express praise: *compliment*    be a good addition: _____

4. opposite of *win*: *lose*    opposite of *tight*: _____

5. not noisy: *quiet*    very: _____

6. come before: *precede*    go forward: _____

7. use time or money: *expend*    grow larger: _____

8. sweet dish: *dessert*    dry place: _____

9. put something somewhere: *set*    rest with bended knees: _____

10. suggestion: *advice*    give advice: _____

11. group of advisors: *council*    give advice: _____

12. move upwards: *rise*    lift up: _____

**EXERCISE 7**    As in Exercise 6, write the missing member of each commonly confused pair of words that you studied in Chapter 6.

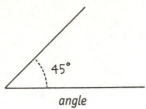

*angle*

1. where two lines meet: *angle*    being from heaven: _____

2. not including: *except*    approve: _____

3. ready to happen: *imminent*    well known: _____

4. comparative of *far: farther*    additional: _____

5. leave a country: *emigrate*    enter a country: _____

6. complete: *thorough*    in one side and out the other: _____

7. take legal responsibility for: *adopt*    change: _____

8. promise: *assure*    make sure: _____

9. put something somewhere: *lay*    rest horizontally: _____

10. result: *effect*    influence: _____

11. feeling of right and wrong: *conscience*    awake: _____

**EXERCISE 8**    Write the American spellings for these British words following the examples presented in Chapter 9.

1. fibre _____    9. learnt _____

2. harbour _____    10. checque _____

3. connexion _____    11. defence _____

4. organise _____    12. neighbour _____

5. programme _____    13. realise _____

6. licence _____    14. analyse _____

7. metre _____    15. humour _____

8. favourite _____    16. aeroplane _____

**EXERCISE 9**    Write the abbreviations, as presented in Chapter 7, for the following words.

1. Tuesday  _____       14. Square  _____

2. Street  _____        15. Wednesday  _____

3. February  _____      16. October  _____

4. in the morning  _____  17. Court  _____

5. Saturday  _____      18. Lane  _____

6. Place  _____         19. Thursday  _____

7. November  _____      20. August  _____

8. Highway  _____       21. April  _____

9. in the afternoon  _____  22. Drive  _____

10. Sunday  _____       23. Terrace  _____

11. January  _____      24. Monday  _____

12. Route  _____        25. before Christ  _____

13. Parkway  _____      26. in the Christian era  _____

**EXERCISE 10**    Write the words for these symbols as presented in Chapter 8.

1. %  _____         10. =  _____

2. @  _____         11. >  _____

3. ×  _____         12. ¢  _____

4. &  _____         13. ≈  _____

5. $  _____         14. /  _____

6. +  _____             _____

7. #  _____             _____

   _____            15. −  _____

8. c/o  _____            _____

9. <  _____          16. ÷  _____

**EXERCISE 11**    Rewrite the words, using hyphens (-) to show where they might be divided at the ends of lines. If a word cannot be divided, write "no." Follow the rules presented in Chapter 7.

1. moreover  _____      6. frequently  _____

2. butter  _____        7. encyclopedia  _____

3. cookbook  _____      8. parallel  _____

4. weight  _____        9. organization  _____

5. package  _____       10. only  _____

**EXERCISE 12**

Rewrite the phrases, adding hyphens as needed by applying the guidelines in Chapter 6. Do not change the word order. If no hyphens are needed, write "none."

1. a two year rental agreement _____

2. nineteenth century philosophy _____

3. a five dollar bill _____

4. a restaurant that is highly recommended _____

5. a well known fact _____

6. a seven year old girl _____

7. an eighty year old _____

8. a battery powered radio _____

9. two hundred forty three _____

10. stone ground flour _____

11. a report of thirty pages _____

12. an air conditioned office _____

**EXERCISE 13**

Complete the words by adding *ei* or *ie* as presented in Chapter 9.

1. for _____ _____ gn

2. _____ _____ ther

3. rec _____ _____ ve

4. gr _____ _____ ve

5. s _____ _____ ze

6. w _____ _____ ght

7. c _____ _____ ling

8. perc _____ _____ ve

9. ch _____ _____ f

10. forf _____ _____ t

**EXERCISE 14**

Complete the words by adding *a* or *e* as presented in Chapter 9.

1. experi _____ nce

2. viol _____ nce

3. attend _____ nce

4. insur _____ nce

5. consci _____ nce

6. abs _____ nce

7. relev _____ nce

8. coincid _____ nce

9. occurr _____ nce

10. perform _____ nce

**EXERCISE 15**

Complete the words by adding double letters, as presented in Chapter 9.

1. o _____ _____ onent

2. fulfi _____ _____

3. a _____ _____ re _____ _____

4. reco _____ _____ end

5. po _____ _____ e _____ _____ ion

6. a _____ _____ umulate

7. guarant _____ _____

8. r _____ _____ _____ _____ ate

9. o _____ _____ asiona _____ _____ y

10. a _____ _____ o _____ _____ odate

**EXERCISE 16** | Proofread the passage, crossing out all errors of types presented in Chapters 6–9. Write the correct spelling above the errors.

sundial

hourglass

The first human beings probably did not concieve of a need to know the exact time. They surely used the sun in the sky to tell the time of day. Their experiance told them when the day was going to begin or end. This method was very inperfect, however, because looking at the sun directly is very dangerous. As civilization preceded, other ways had to be found. Two early inventions made a big diference in humans' ability to tell time and made organising their activities around specific times a real posibility.

About 3500 b.c., the Egyptians began developing sundials, which showed the angel of the sun by casting shadows on the ground or on other objects. Looking at shadows was a lot better for the eyes then looking into the sky. There were still problems, however, because the son is sometimes covered by quiet large clouds, and of course, at night it cannot be seen at all.

At about the same time sundials were being developed, the first hourglasses were constructed in the form of water clocks. Water dripped thorough a hole in the bottom of a bowl, and the acumulation of water in a lower bowl told the time. Water clocks, however, could not be used in freezing weather. Later, sand was used, but because of sand's wieght, large hourglasses could not be transported. Smaller ones were used for measuring small amounts of time.

Both the sundial and hourglass are kronometers—devices for measuring time. Niether of them is very accurate, but because they fulfiled the purpose for which they were intended much better then anything that had come before them, they were important developments in the teknology of telling time.

**ERCISE 17** | Proofread the items, crossing out all errors of types presented in Chapters 6–9. Write the correct spellings above the errors.

1. According to the National Safety Counsel, most acidental deaths in the United States involve motor vehicles, such as cars and trucks. Falls are the next most frequent cause of acidental death.

2. In the past, people engaged in correspondance with friends and relatives primarily by writing letters. Today, many more people rely on the conveniance of e-mail to maintain contact in writing. With the assistance of e-mail, they can send and recieve written communications imediately.

3. Many Americans are concerned about our dependance on foriegn oil to power our vehicles. These people believe that more research into alternatives such as solar powered cars may find the answer to our energy needs.

4. The United States is one of the few nations to use measurements such as yards and quarts. Most countries now use metres, litres, and other metric measurements. The American preferance for the older system is based on costume and tradition. Also, after thinking of your hieght in feet and inches all your life, it's very difficult to concieve of it in other terms.

5. 233 So. Green Str.

6. 555 We. Hanover Dve.

7. 312 No. Lindley Av., Apart. 67

8. 1905 E. Oak Ro.

9. 74 Norwich Pce.

10. 88 Holland Boul.

**Spelling Word Bank**   In the Spelling Word Bank at the end of this book, write words from this chapter that you find especially difficult or interesting or that are especially good examples.

# POST-TEST

Do you remember this test? Take it again. Make a check mark (✓) in the appropriate column according to how you feel about your answer: "SURE" or "NOT SURE."

**A.** Make new words by combining the roots and the suffixes, as indicated.

|  |  | **SURE** | **NOT SURE** |
|---|---|---|---|
| 1. study + ing | _____ | _____ | _____ |
| 2. happen + ed | _____ | _____ | _____ |
| 3. lonely + ness | _____ | _____ | _____ |
| 4. occur + ing | _____ | _____ | _____ |
| 5. continue + ing | _____ | _____ | _____ |
| 6. swim + er | _____ | _____ | _____ |

**B.** Write new words by adding the suffix *−er* or *−or* to each word.

|  |  | **SURE** | **NOT SURE** |
|---|---|---|---|
| 1. process | _____ | _____ | _____ |
| 2. translate | _____ | _____ | _____ |
| 3. perform | _____ | _____ | _____ |
| 4. observe | _____ | _____ | _____ |

**C.** Complete each word by adding the suffx *−yze,* *−ise,* or *−ize.*

|  |  | **SURE** | **NOT SURE** |
|---|---|---|---|
| 1. real | _____ | _____ | _____ |
| 2. organ | _____ | _____ | _____ |
| 3. surpr | _____ | _____ | _____ |
| 4. paral | _____ | _____ | _____ |

**D.** Write the American spelling for each of these British words.

|  |  | **SURE** | **NOT SURE** |
|---|---|---|---|
| 1. centre | _____ | _____ | _____ |
| 2. behaviour | _____ | _____ | _____ |
| 3. programme | _____ | _____ | _____ |
| 4. defence | _____ | _____ | _____ |

**E.** Circle the letter of the correct phrase.

|  |  | SURE | NOT SURE |
|---|---|---|---|
| 1. a. a forty-years-old man | b. a forty-year-old man | _____ | _____ |
| 2. a. one-and-one-half hours | b. one and one-half hours | _____ | _____ |
| 3. a. a well-known man | b. a well known man | _____ | _____ |
| 4. a. a man who's well-known | b. a man who's well known | _____ | _____ |

**F.** Circle the letter of the word that is correctly spelled.

|  |  | SURE | NOT SURE |
|---|---|---|---|
| 1. a. gorgeous | b. gorgous | _____ | _____ |
| 2. a. mysteryous | b. mysterious | _____ | _____ |
| 3. a. outrageous | b. outragous | _____ | _____ |
| 4. a. ambitous | b. ambitious | _____ | _____ |
| 5. a. conceive | b. concieve | _____ | _____ |
| 6. a. exaggerate | b. exagerate | _____ | _____ |
| 7. a. maintenance | b. maintenence | _____ | _____ |
| 8. a. referance | b. reference | _____ | _____ |
| 9. a. imoral | b. immoral | _____ | _____ |
| 10. a. misspell | b. mispell | _____ | _____ |
| 11. a. unecessary | b. unnecessary | _____ | _____ |
| 12. a. missconduct | b. misconduct | _____ | _____ |

**G.** Write new words by adding −*able* or −*ible*.

|  |  | SURE | NOT SURE |
|---|---|---|---|
| 1. notice | _____ | _____ | _____ |
| 2. vis | _____ | _____ | _____ |
| 3. accept | _____ | _____ | _____ |
| 4. elig | _____ | _____ | _____ |

**H.** Write new words by adding −*ion*.

|  |  | SURE | NOT SURE |
|---|---|---|---|
| 1. divide | _____ | _____ | _____ |
| 2. satisfy | _____ | _____ | _____ |
| 3. submit | _____ | _____ | _____ |
| 4. expand | _____ | _____ | _____ |

**I.** Write the plurals of these singular nouns.

|  |  | SURE | NOT SURE |
|---|---|---|---|
| 1. nucleus | _____ | _____ | _____ |
| 2. medium | _____ | _____ | _____ |
| 3. phenomenon | _____ | _____ | _____ |
| 4. crisis | _____ | _____ | _____ |

**J.** Write the abbreviations for these words.

|  |  | SURE | NOT SURE |
|---|---|---|---|
| 1. Avenue | _____ | _____ | _____ |
| 2. Thursday | _____ | _____ | _____ |
| 3. after noon | _____ | _____ | _____ |
| 4. Apartment | _____ | _____ | _____ |

**K.** Rewrite the words, using hyphens (-) to indicate where the words could be divided at the end of a line.

|  |  | SURE | NOT SURE |
|---|---|---|---|
| 1. explained | _____ | _____ | _____ |
| 2. identify | _____ | _____ | _____ |
| 3. blackboard | _____ | _____ | _____ |
| 4. running | _____ | _____ | _____ |

**L.** Use apostrophes (') to express these phrases in a different way.

|  | SURE | NOT SURE |
|---|---|---|

1. book of the student

_____    _____    _____

2. house of the boys

_____    _____    _____

3. work of the women

_____    _____    _____

4. job of James

_____    _____    _____

**M.** Combine two roots for each item to make a word with the given meaning. Example: study of the stars = astrology.

| | | SURE | NOT SURE |
|---|---|---|---|
| 1. study of time: | _____ | _____ | _____ |
| 2. distant sound: | _____ | _____ | _____ |
| 3. heat measurer: | _____ | _____ | _____ |
| 4. light writing: | _____ | _____ | _____ |

Now, look at the pretest you took in Chapter 1, and write the number of items you checked "SURE" and "NOT SURE" in the spaces provided. Then, enter the number of items you checked "SURE" and "NOT SURE" for the post-test. The number of "SURE" items should be larger now. There are a total of 62 items.

| | SURE | NOT SURE |
|---|---|---|
| Pretest | _____ | _____ |
| Post-test | _____ | _____ |

Discuss the correct answers with your instructor. Compare your answers on the pre- and post-tests. Write your scores below. The number of correct answers should be larger for the post-test.

| | **Number correct** |
|---|---|
| Pretest | _____ |
| Post-test | _____ |

Identify any problem areas that remain, and go back in your book to review the relevant sections and chapters.

# APPENDIX A

## IRREGULAR VERBS*

| Simple Form | Past | Past Participle | Simple Form | Past | Past Participle |
|---|---|---|---|---|---|
| be | was, were | been | grind | ground | ground |
| beat | beat | beat | grow | grew | grown |
| become | became | become | hang | hung | hung |
| begin | began | begun | have | had | had |
| bend | bent | bent | hear | heard | heard |
| bet | bet | bet | hide | hid | hidden |
| bite | bit | bitten | hit | hit | hit |
| bleed | bled | bled | hold | held | held |
| blow | blew | blown | hurt | hurt | hurt |
| break | broke | broken | keep | kept | kept |
| breed | bred | bred | kneel | knelt | knelt |
| bring | brought | brought | know | knew | known |
| build | built | built | lay | laid | laid |
| burst | burst | burst | lead | led | led |
| buy | bought | bought | leave | left | left |
| catch | caught | caught | lend | lent | lent |
| choose | chose | chosen | let | let | let |
| come | came | come | lie (down) | lay | lain |
| cost | cost | cost | light | lit | lit |
| cut | cut | cut | lose | lost | lost |
| deal | dealt | dealt | make | made | made |
| do | did | done | mean | meant | meant |
| draw | draw | drawn | meet | met | met |
| drink | drank | drunk | pay | paid | paid |
| drive | drove | driven | prove | proved | proven/proved |
| eat | ate | eaten | | | |
| fall | fell | fallen | put | put | put |
| feed | fed | fed | quit | quit | quit |
| feel | felt | felt | read | read | read |
| fight | fought | fought | rid | rid | rid |
| find | found | found | ride | rode | ridden |
| fit | fit | fit | ring | rang | rung |
| flee | fled | fled | rise | rose | risen |
| fly | flew | flown | run | ran | run |
| forget | forgot | forgotten | say | said | said |
| forgive | forgave | forgiven | see | saw | seen |
| freeze | froze | frozen | seek | sought | sought |
| get | got | gotten | sell | sold | sold |
| give | gave | given | send | sent | sent |
| go | went | gone | set | set | set |

*(Continued)*

| Simple Form | Past | Past Participle | Simple Form | Past | Past Participle |
|---|---|---|---|---|---|
| sew | sewed | sewn/sewed | strike | struck | struck |
| shake | shook | shaken | string | strung | strung |
| shine | shone | shone | swear | swore | sworn |
| shoot | shot | shot | sweep | swept | swept |
| show | showed | shown/showed | swell | swelled | swollen/swelled |
| shrink | shrank | shrunk | swim | swam | swum |
| shut | shut | shut | swing | swung | swung |
| sing | sang | sung | take | took | taken |
| sit | sat | sat | teach | taught | taught |
| sleep | slept | slept | tear | tore | torn |
| slide | slid | slid | tell | told | told |
| speak | spoke | spoken | think | thought | thought |
| spend | spent | spent | throw | threw | thrown |
| spin | spun | spun | understand | understood | understood |
| split | split | split | wake | woke | woken |
| spread | spread | spread | wear | wore | worn |
| stand | stood | stood | wet | wet | wet |
| steal | stole | stolen | win | won | won |
| stick | stuck | stuck | wind | wound | wound |
| sting | stung | stung | wring | wrung | wrung |
| stink | stank | stunk | write | wrote | written |

*(Continued)*

# APPENDIX B

## COUNTRIES, NATIONALITIES, AND CAPITALS

| Country | Nationality adjective | Capital |
| --- | --- | --- |
| Afghanistan | Afghan | Kabul |
| Albania | Albanian | Tirana |
| Algeria | Algerian | Algiers |
| Angola | Angolan | Luanda |
| Argentina | Argentinian | Buenos Aires |
| Armenia | Armenian | Yerevan |
| Australia | Australian | Canberra |
| Austria | Austrian | Vienna |
| Azerbaijan | Azerbaijani | Baku |
| Bahrain | Bahraini | Manama |
| Bangladesh | Bangladeshi | Dhaka |
| Belarus | Belarusian | Minsk |
| Belgium | Belgian | Brussels |
| Belize | Belizean | Belmopan |
| Benin | Beninese | Porto-Novo |
| Bhutan | Bhutanese | Thimphu |
| Bosnia and Herzegovina | Bosnian, Herzegovinian | Sarajevo |
| Brazil | Brazilian | Brasilia |
| Bulgaria | Bulgarian | Sofia |
| Burundi | Burundian | Bujumbura |
| Cambodia | Cambodia | Phnom Penh |
| Cameroon | Cameroonian | Yaoundé |
| Canada | Canadian | Ottawa |
| Chad | Chadian | N'Djamena |
| Chile | Chilean | Santiago |
| China | Chinese | Beijing |
| Colombia | Colombian | Bogotá |
| Congo, Democratic Republic of | Congolese | Kinshasa |
| Congo, Republic of | Congolese | Brazzaville |
| Costa Rica | Costa Rican | San José |
| Croatia | Croatian | Zagreb |
| Cuba | Cuban | Havana |
| Czech Republic | Czech | Prague |
| Denmark | Danish | Copenhagen |
| Dominican Republic | Dominican | Santo Domingo |
| Ecuador | Ecuadorian | Quito |
| Egypt | Egyptian | Cairo |
| El Salvador | Salvadoran | San Salvador |
| Estonia | Estonian | Tallinn |
| Ethiopia | Ethiopian | Addis Ababa |
| Finland | Finnish | Helsinki |

*(Continued)*

| Country | Nationality adjective | Capital |
|---|---|---|
| France | French | Paris |
| Georgia | Georgian | Tbilisi |
| Germany | German | Berlin |
| Ghana | Ghanaian | Acera |
| Greece | Greek | Athens |
| Guatemala | Guatemalan | Guatemala City |
| Haiti | Haitian | Port-au-Prince |
| Honduras | Honduran | Tegucigalpa |
| Hungary | Hungarian | Budapest |
| Iceland | Icelandic | Reykjavik |
| India | Indian | New Delhi |
| Indonesia | Indonesian | Jakarta |
| Iran | Iranian | Tehran |
| Iraq | Iraqi | Baghdad |
| Ireland | Irish | Dublin |
| Israel | Israeli | Jerusalem |
| Italy | Italian | Rome |
| Japan | Japanese | Tokyo |
| Jordan | Jordanian | Amman |
| Kazakstan | Kazakstani | Almaty |
| Kenya | Kenyan | Nairobi |
| Kuwait | Kuwaiti | Kuwait |
| Laos | Laotian | Vientiane |
| Latvia | Latvian | Riga |
| Lebanon | Lebanese | Beirut |
| Liberia | Liberian | Monrovia |
| Libya | Libyan | Tripoli |
| Lithuania | Lithuanian | Vilnius |
| Macedonia | Macedonian | Skopje |
| Madagascar | Malagasy, Madagascan | Antananarivo |
| Malaysia | Malaysian | Kuala Lumpur |
| Mexico | Mexican | Mexico City |
| Mongolia | Mongolian | Ulan Bator |
| Morocco | Moroccan | Rabat |
| Mozambique | Mozambican | Maputo |
| Myanmar | Burmese | Yangon |
| Nepal | Nepalese | Katmandu |
| Netherlands, the | Dutch | Amsterdam |
| New Zealand | New Zealander | Wellington |
| Nicaragua | Nicaraguan | Managua |
| Niger | Nigerien | Niamey |
| Nigeria | Nigerian | Abuja |
| Norway | Norwegian | Oslo |
| North Korea | North Korean | Pyongyang |
| Oman | Omani | Muscat |
| Pakistan | Pakistani | Islamabad |
| Panama | Panamanian | Panama City |
| Papua New Guinea | Papua New Guinean | Port Moresby |
| Paraguay | Paraguayan | Asunción |
| Peru | Peruvian | Lima |
| Philippines | Filipino | Manila |
| Poland | Polish | Warsaw |
| Portugal | Portuguese | Lisbon |

*(Continued)*

| Country | Nationality adjective | Capital |
|---|---|---|
| Romania | Romanian | Bucharest |
| Russia | Russian | Moscow |
| Rwanda | Rwandan | Kigali |
| Saudi Arabia | Saudi Arabian | Riyadh |
| Senegal | Senegalese | Dakar |
| Serbia and Montenegro | Serbian, Montenegrin | Belgrade |
| Sierra Leone | Sierra Leonean | Freetown |
| Singapore | Singaporean | Singapore |
| Slovakia | Slovakian | Bratislava |
| Somalia | Somali | Mogadishu |
| South Africa | South African | Pretoria |
| South Korea | South Korean | Seoul |
| Spain | Spanish | Madrid |
| Sri Lanka | Sri Lankan | Colombo |
| Sudan | Sudanese | Khartoum |
| Sweden | Swedish | Stockholm |
| Switzerland | Swiss | Bern |
| Syria | Syrian | Damascus |
| Taiwan | Taiwanese | Taipei |
| Tajikistan | Tajik | Dushanbe |
| Thailand | Thai | Bangkok |
| Tunisia | Tunisian | Tunis |
| Turkey | Turkish | Ankara |
| Uganda | Ugandan | Kampala |
| Ukraine | Ukrainian | Kiev |
| United Arab Emirates, the | Erimiant | Abu Dhabi |
| United Kingdom, the | British | London |
| United States of America, the | American | Washington, D.C. |
| Uruguay | Uruguayan | Montevideo |
| Uzbekistan | Uzbek | Tashkent |
| Venezuela | Venezuelan | Caracas |
| Vietnam | Vietnamese | Hanoi |
| Yemen | Yemeni | San'a |
| Zambia | Zambian | Lusaka |
| Zimbabwe | Zimbabwean | Harare |

# APPENDIX C

## STATES OF THE UNITED STATES, CAPITALS, AND POSTAL ABBREVIATIONS

| State | Capital | Postal abbreviation | State | Capital | Postal abbreviation |
|---|---|---|---|---|---|
| Alabama | Montgomery | AL | Montana | Helena | MT |
| Alaska | Juneau | AK | Nebraska | Lincoln | NE |
| Arizona | Phoenix | AZ | Nevada | Carson City | NV |
| Arkansas | Little Rock | AR | New Hampshire | Concord | NH |
| California | Sacramento | CA | New Jersey | Trenton | NJ |
| Colorado | Denver | CO | New Mexico | Santa Fe | NM |
| Connecticut | Hartford | CT | New York | Albany | NY |
| Delaware | Dover | DE | North Carolina | Raleigh | NC |
| Florida | Tallahassee | FL | North Dakota | Bismarck | ND |
| Georgia | Atlanta | GA | Ohio | Columbus | OH |
| Hawaii | Honolulu | HI | Oklahoma | Oklahoma City | OK |
| Idaho | Boise | ID | Oregon | Salem | OR |
| Illinois | Springfield | IL | Pennsylvania | Harrisburg | PA |
| Indiana | Indianapolis | IN | Rhode Island | Providence | RI |
| Iowa | Des Moines | IA | South Carolina | Columbia | SC |
| Kansas | Topeka | KS | South Dakota | Pierre | SD |
| Kentucky | Frankfort | KY | Tennessee | Nashville | TN |
| Louisiana | Baton Rouge | LA | Texas | Austin | TX |
| Maine | Augusta | ME | Utah | Salt Lake City | UT |
| Maryland | Annapolis | MD | Vermont | Montpelier | VT |
| Massachusetts | Boston | MA | Virginia | Richmond | VA |
| Michigan | Lansing | MI | Washington | Olympia | WA |
| Minnesota | St. Paul | MN | West Virginia | Charleston | WV |
| Mississippi | Jackson | MS | Wisconsin | Madison | WI |
| Missouri | Jefferson City | MO | Wyoming | Cheyenne | WY |

| Territories | Capital | Postal abbreviation |
|---|---|---|
| Guam | Agana | GU |
| Puerto Rico | San Juan | PR |
| Virgin Islands | Charlotte Amalie | VI |

# SPELLING WORD BANK

On these pages, write words that you find especially difficult or interesting or that are especially good examples of their type.

**CHAPTER 1**

**CHAPTER 2**

**CHAPTER 3**

# CHAPTER 4

# CHAPTER 5

# REVIEW OF CHAPTERS 2–5

# CHAPTER 6

**CHAPTER 7**

**CHAPTER 8**

**CHAPTER 9**

**REVIEW OF CHAPTERS 6–9**